TWO WAYS *to* TRAVEL

REV. NORMAN E. MOON

TWO WAYS TO TRAVEL

Published by Revival Nation Publishing

Softcover ISBN 978-1-926625-00-3
eBook ISBN 978-1-926625-09-6

Printed in the United States of America

Revival Nation Publishing
Ontario • CANADA

P.O. Box 30001
RPO Eastland Plaza
Sarnia, Ontario
N7T 0A7

www.RevivalNationPublishing.com
1-866-487-1361

TWO WAYS *to* TRAVEL

DEDICATION

I find myself in a place I thought I would never be. I got here because I grew tired of seeing opportunity; blessing and anointing pass me by. With a lot of help, I decided to step out into the unknown and capture the prize. I began to see that God had provided what I needed, but like the children of Israel, I had to go in and possess it. The possession, however, would never have taken place without the help of certain circumstances and people!

Circumstances have brought experience to my life. Many times I have cried out, "Lord why is this happening to me?" There has been a lot of pain in my life, but pain became a stepping-stone to greatness. You might ask, "How?" Well, I've made pain reimburse me! I chose to make it surrender lessons that made me better than I was before. I found out how it worked and discovered how to overcome it. Stripping it of its numbing effects, I used it to climb victoriously, through faith in my Savior, Jesus Christ!

I have had both wonderful and hurtful people in my life. Some have helped me by believing in me. Others have wounded me in ways that could have destroyed me. They meant it for evil, but God used it for good. Through faith, I turned the scars into maps to take me to my destination. To both the wonderful and the hurtful people in my life, I say, "Thank you! Without you there would be no me."

A special thanks goes to my wife, Debbie, who has been my greatest ally and critic. There have been times when I couldn't go another step. Then I would hear her saying, "Come on you can make it! The kids and I believe in you." At other times, she would, on purpose, make me angry, saying I should just quit! She would goad me on to action by declaring that I wasn't man enough to finish what I had started. She has always known just what to say, and the perfect time to say it, motivating me to see that I was more than a conqueror through Christ. My wife and my best friend for more than 39 years, I thank you for being you. Love you!

I want to thank my boys: Eric, Aaron, Anthony and Michael, all men now and great supporters of their old man. Eric, who has gone on to be with the Lord, has been a great inspiration to me because he beat the odds. He was born with cerebral palsy, but did everything he wanted to do, until he passed away. He would not be denied.

Aaron, now the oldest, is a man of strength. He didn't have a regular childhood because he was always taking on the role of protector for his brother. He is a rock on whom you can always depend.

Anthony is the visionary. He sees things that others don't and attempts to conquer them, after much thought and calculation of course. Anthony has been a great motivator in this project and I thank him.

Michael, my youngest, has taught his old man how to pray and have faith. Michael has given me a lot of illustrations over the years, for some of them, I say thanks! He's a young man with mountains of potential, but like me, he must break the lock on what is already his, in order to benefit from it. I am very proud of all my sons!

I'd also like to thank my daughters-in-law. Without them, this project wouldn't be complete: Belle, my reading and laughing buddy, who shows such great compassion to those that hurt. Helen, for her contribution of class and honesty, when decisions on the book needed to be made. Tatyana, who has helped me stay focused and inspired me to creatively color out side the box.

To my River of Life church family, my deepest thanks for all your support and encouragement. Without you, this wouldn't have been possible.

I want to thank Charlie Martinez and George Williamson, who, for years, have been my accountability partners helping me to stay on track.

I would like to thank Jackie Cooper (www.jackiecooperwriter.com), who did a fantastic job writing the preface to each section of the book, as well as helping me organize my thoughts and words on paper. Our partnership has been great and I truly appreciate her input and support during this process. I look forward to working with her again in the future to reach a lost world for Jesus Christ.

'Thank you' as well to Vivian Gutierrez for taking the time to provide us with a fresh set of educated eyes to review the project. I appreciate your continued friendship and dedication to helping others see there is hope through Jesus Christ.

Lastly, I thank my Mom and Dad (Frances and Alonzo), who were good parents. They allowed their children to stand on their shoulders, to get a better look at what was possible in this world. My mother-In-law, Bessie Virden, for her help, friendship and moral support through the years, thanks, Mom!

My brothers and sisters… what a ride we all have had! I love them deeply. I feel gratitude for my family history, which has blended the strength of the Moon and Griffin families. Thank you all!

ABOUT
Two Ways To Travel

This book has been written as a wake-up call for everyone who feels trapped by the circumstances of life. The main objective is to help you see that while you're alive, there's hope. God's well aware of you and He wants to help you. Not only right now, to get you out of the hole you may be in. That's important; but more importantly He wants to help you from getting into holes in the future. He wants to provide meaning, depth, joy and reward in your life.

One of God's names is 'the God who hears'. The Bible says that He knows every hair on your head. In fact, each one is numbered. You lose one, He knows.

You may have thought that He was to blame for a lot that's gone wrong in your life or the lives of people you know. It's a common misconception. Sometimes even preached in churches. This book is here to tell you that it's not true. It's a lie of the devil meant to keep you in bondage, and away from God – the One who can, and will help you.

My prayer is that this is an opportunity for the Holy Spirit to minister hope, healing and wholeness to you. In Jeremiah 29:11 it says:

"For I know the thoughts and plans that I have for you, says the Lord, thoughts and plans for welfare and peace and not for evil, to give you

hope in your final outcome."

May you be blessed in reading this book and get to know Jesus better through it.

- *Pastor Norman E. Moon*

Table of Contents

PART ONE
Two Ways To Travel

"I was terrified. It wasn't that the storm was the worst I'd seen. I'm a fisherman. I'm used to the foul tricks of the wind and waves. But that night was awful. Remembering makes me shudder. I truly thought we wouldn't make it.

Peter, James, John, Andrew and I, were in Peter's boat. We were on our way to the other side, as the Master had ordered. We hadn't gone very far when the storm hit, slowing us down. We were already exhausted. It'd been a long, amazing, thrilling day. Five thousand men, plus who knows how many women and children fed with just five loaves and two fish meant for a young boy. It was freaky. Our exhaustion was caused more by emotion than anything physical.

At any rate, we just didn't have our usual spunk. It was the fourth watch of the night, I was the first one to notice and raise the alarm. I grabbed Peter's arm and yelled above the storm, "WHAT is that!?" He just stared. Didn't say anything, but I could tell he was rattled. Before long everyone was at the side, gazing in horror. I was afraid the boat would tip. I could see the others were just as scared as I was. There it was, a white apparition floating toward us over the water. I heard a keening in the air and realized it was me... screaming, only I could barely hear it, "It's a ghost! Oh God! It's a ghost! Oh God! Save us! Save us!"

Peter shook me. "Shut up! Get a grip! Thomas, get a grip!" Then he turned back toward the rapidly approaching apparition, yelling, "JESUS!" We heard the Master's calm voice," Take courage! I AM. Stop being afraid!" The authority was unmistakable. Peter's eyes were sharper than mine, but still, how could we be sure...? We'd left the Master on the bank and how could He possibly walk on water!? Only ghosts could do that. Not real men!

Suddenly I heard Peter roar, "Lord! If it's You, tell me to come to you on the water!" My jaw dropped. Was he MAD? Did Peter realize what he was asking? What if it was a ghost...? The apparition with the Lord's voice replied, "Come." Just 'come'. I wanted to throw up as Peter vaulted over the side of the boat. That was the end of him, I thought. Then, I couldn't believe my eyes! Instead of being swallowed up by the waves, Peter was walking as if on dry land. Men were gasping. James was praying, sobbing. I was making some unearthly sound.

Peter, stomping towards Jesus as cocky as you please, within a few feet of Him, when suddenly, as if he only now saw the wind and waves around him, hesitated, then slowly, began to sink. Water rose behind him, about to smother him. Above the tumult, Peter screamed, "Lord, save me!" Jesus, reached out, grasping Peter firmly. "Oh ye of little faith, why did you doubt?" echoed clearly over the sea, now strangely calm. Jesus led Peter into the boat. The wind stopped. Just like that.

Drenched with brine, tears and fear, in dread and wonder at the Son of God in our midst, we fell to our knees worshipping Him. What else could we do? We'd fallen short. We knew it. He knew. But, He still loved us. He knew everything in our hearts. We could only accept His mercy and loving kindness. "

CHAPTER 1
Natural or Supernatural - It's Your Choice

If you're tired of being a victim of the storms of life, this message will rank as one of the most important you'll ever read.

There are two ways to travel through life. The natural way you're accustomed to, or the supernatural way I'm going to tell you about.

When Jesus Christ walked this earth in the flesh, his disciples learned first hand about the difference. It's that difference that I want to show you today. Take a look at what the Bible says about one of those times when the difference between natural and supernatural amazed Jesus' own disciples:

"And when the disciples saw him walking on the sea, ***they were troubled, saying, It is a spirit; and they cried out for fear****. But straightway Jesus spake unto them, saying, Be of good cheer; it is I; be not afraid.*

And Peter answered him and said, Lord, if it be thou; bid me come unto thee on the water. And he said, Come. And when Peter was come down out of the ship, he walked on the water, to go to Jesus. ***But when he saw the wind boisterous, he was afraid; and beginning to sink, he cried, saying, Lord, save me.***

And immediately Jesus stretched forth his hand, and caught him, and said unto him, ***O thou of little faith, wherefore didst thou doubt?*** *And when they were come into the ship, the wind ceased. Then they that were in the ship came and worshipped him, saying, Of a truth thou art the Son of God"* (Matthew 14:26-33).

You can travel two ways through life: in the boat, like the disciples did, or walking on water like Jesus did. Now, stay with me here. First of all, I want you to notice the behavior inside the boat. Take a look at those disciples. They were troubled. They weren't just troubled, they were seeing ghosts! They looked out on that water and saw Jesus, but they thought He was a ghost. They didn't recognize Him.

Do you know what I'm talking about? Has that ever happened to you? It's like some of those old films we used to watch. Someone would see a ghost and their eyeballs would get as big as cue balls and they'd run through a wall, all because they *thought* they saw a ghost. Now this is just the kind of behavior that was going on in that boat. Those men were full of fear. They were crying and hollering. All because they *thought* they saw a ghost.

Living the 'boat life' will keepyou from getting to the other side.

If you read Matthew 14:22, you'll see that these men were in the boat because they were going somewhere. They were going where Jesus had told them to go. He said, "Go to the other side." They had a destination. They were to go to the other side. Not anywhere else. To the other side. Now, if Jesus tells you to go to the other side then He wants you to *get* to the other side.

And if Jesus tells you to go to the other side and you do what He tells you, you can be sure you're going to get to the other side.

Take a look at how Jesus behaves. He's in the same storm as the disciples. But He says, "Be not afraid." He says, "You men are in this storm. But don't be afraid. Don't be fearful. Don't begin to act in fear."

What He's also saying is "Don't be scared away from what I've told you to do. Don't be scared away from reaching the other side. I want you on the other side. *I want you to accomplish that which I've told you to do.*" He's saying, "I want you to *do what I've told you to do.* I want you *on the other side.* Don't stop in the middle of the sea or go to the left or to the right of the sea. I want you to go to the other side." So He gives them this one, simple instruction, "Be not afraid."

Do you know what's keeping you from experiencing the blessing of God today? It's the very same thing that was trying to keep the disciples from getting to the other side. It's fear. Yes, fear.

God has promised us great things. But fear tries to stop us from getting what God has promised us. And when you have fear, you'll also have confusion. And when you have fear *and* confusion, they bring in a lot of other things. When you get scared you start thinking, "I can't do this."

All fear and confusion create road-blocks that try to stop you from getting where you want to go. They're detours. And if you take them, you'll end up going somewhere other than your destination. They'll stop you from getting to the other side.

Take another look at the disciples. They're in the boat. They're scared out of their wits. All except for Peter, who decides to get out of the boat to be where Jesus is. They're living the 'boat life', if you will, and it has tentacles like an octopus.

How often have you lived the 'boat life'? When you're in the boat, you and everyone around you is afraid. Everyone's talking negatively. Everyone's telling everyone else all about their troubles.

Have you ever been around people like that? Sure you have. You come into the room and you're all excited and happy. Then you sit next to somebody 'in the boat' and in five minutes you are bummed out! You come out of there and you're thinking, "Man, life *is* bad, isn't it? Boy, things are *stinking* today! Things are really out of kilter. Nothing's right. What *else* could happen in my life?"

You see, that boat has tentacles that will *pull you back* into the 'boat life' if you don't make up your mind to *stay out*!

The disciples in the boat were complaining. They were afraid. They were saying many negative things about what was keeping them from getting to the other side. They didn't believe they would make it to their destination. And while they're seeing what they believe is the 'ghost', they're not paddling the boat! These men have stopped their journey in the middle of the sea. They're looking at the storm, not paddling the boat. They're not doing anything except sitting there crying and being afraid. They're not doing anything. Just like some of us. We've stopped in the middle of life and we're not doing anything because the tentacles of the 'boat life' have pulled us back in.

I want you to see something here: everybody goes through storms. How you travel is up to you. It's a choice. You can stay in the boat with the fear, or you can walk across the water with Jesus.

CHAPTER 2
Choosing to Travel Supernaturally

Everyone goes through storms. Perhaps you're going through a storm today. If not, you almost certainly have gone through one in the past, and you'll most certainly go through more in the future.

The point isn't whether you go through storms, but how you go through them. We all go through hard times, but not all of us get to the other side. Some of us get lost in the middle of the sea. And some of us just barely get to the other side, but in what state?

Some of us haven't even got onto the sea yet. We're still hanging around on the side, waiting to push off into the sea. Some of us are paddling around in circles, in the middle of the sea and we find ourselves in the storm. We aren't getting anywhere. But God told you to go to the other side. Jesus will go to the other side. Now look at how Jesus gets there.

Travel without fear:

The first way that Jesus gets to the other side is by traveling without fear. Have you ever thought about how stupid fear is? I'm not talking about the kind of fear that says, "Don't point that gun at me." Or when someone says, "Don't put your hand on the hot stove" or "Don't cross the road when the light is green for the traffic." That's what helps us survive. Those are normal, common-sense things to keep us from harm. But, when you think about it, you can see how stupid real fear is. Real fear tells you things like someone's outside when there's no one there.

Fear has you scared when there's no reason to be scared. Fear tells you that something's going to happen when nine times out of ten, nothing happens. How many times have you been fearful about something that hadn't yet happened … and never did? Fear lies to you. Fear is a liar from the pit of hell. It's a tool of the devil. The devil says, "You're never going to make it. You'll never make it to the other side."

But, if Jesus told you to go to the other side, then that's where you're going to go. The devil can't stop you.

The devil tells you that you can't get to the other side because you're stupid. He says you can't get to the other side because you're scared. You can't get to the other side because you don't have the right kind of boat.

Well, let me tell you that the only way you *won't* get to the other side is if you listen to all these lies. Listening to and believing the devil's lies, stops us from accomplishing things because we're functioning on a lie instead of the truth. The truth is: you're going to the other side.

Using the storm to get you to the other side…

Jesus traveled walking on the water. The men in the boat are fighting the water. Jesus is walking ON TOP of the trouble…He's on His way to the other side. Are you doing that? Are you walking ON TOP of the trouble to the other side, or are you with the men in the boat fighting the water? What I want you to see is that everyone goes through trouble. It's up to you how you go through it. You can use that trouble to get over to the other side. Let me explain:

You can walk ON TOP of that trouble – that very same trouble that tried to put you in fear, so that you'd believe you wouldn't make it! This is what I mean. Do you know that eagles ride storms? Do you know what that means? The eagle gets ON TOP of the storm. They use that storm. They make that storm work for them.

They use the same air currents that could blow them into destruction to *lift them up and carry them over the turmoil*! They use those currents to take them to their destination instead of staying in the middle of it and letting it *keep* them from their destination. Most of us don't do that. We let the very thing that we could use to get us to our destination destroy us instead. We let it get on top of us, instead of us getting on top of it.

Look at Luke 4:24-30. Jesus had just read the scripture from Isaiah that told of His coming to set the captives free. He anticipated their lack of faith in Him and commented:

> *"And He said, Verily I say unto you, No prophet is accepted in his own country. But I tell you of a truth, many widows were in Israel in the days of Elias, when the heaven was shut up three years and six months, when great famine was throughout all the land; but unto none of them was Elias sent, save unto Sarepta, a city of Sidon, unto a woman that was a widow. And many lepers were in Israel in the time of Eliseus the prophet; and none of them was cleansed, saving Naaman the Syrian. And all they in the synagogue, when they heard these things, were filled with wrath, and rose up, and thrust him out of the city, and led him unto the brow of the hill whereon their city was built, that they might cast him down headlong.* ***But he passing through the midst of them went his way,"***

The very crowd bent on destroying Jesus could not touch him because his boldness confused them. He was in the midst of them, but they couldn't pin-point where he was. The Bible says it wasn't His time to die. Well, neither is it your time, so live!

Another example is found in Acts 23:6. Paul is on trial by a council of Pharisees and Sadducees. However, he escapes their clutches by highlighting an issue of contention between the sects. Violence erupts and the Roman guards remove Paul for fear that he would be torn to pieces.

We could go on and on with examples of how God can help people by using seemingly adverse conditions to their benefit. There is a way to victory, but you have to have the eyes of faith to see and act on it!

Get out of the boat

Jesus didn't let the storm stop His progress. He stepped out on that water and began to walk. When Peter saw Him, he got out of the boat and they were walking together. They were moving over those waves and nothing was stopping them.

While Peter kept his eyes on Jesus, and while he believed he could walk on water, because Jesus said, "Come" he was fine. He walked on top of the same waves that had the rest of men in the boat terrified. But then Peter looked at the waves. The 'boat life' tentacles were reaching out to pull him back. He became afraid and the boat looked like the only safe place.

I'm going to tell you something though: inside the boat is the worst place you can be. That's where defeat is. The boat is the place where you don't get your needs met.

Staying in that boat means never seeing the glory and the power that God has for you when you step out and do what He's told you to do.

Because, when you're living in the boat, living that 'boat life' you're in fear. You're in pain.

You're in turmoil. The 'boat life' makes you doubt even those things that are sure in your life.

Fear makes you doubt even what you're sure of

Think about it. Those men in the boat were fishermen. Come on now! They're fishermen! They're on the water all the time. They've been in storms before. But fear made them doubt something they'd been sure of all their lives. That's what the devil does. He makes you afraid and unsure of things you already know. That's how fear works. That's how the 'boat life' works. It dominates your life. It will dominate it more and more and more and get bigger and bigger to the point where it will stop you from doing anything you've planned, or that God has told you to do.

Not too long ago, I watched a documentary about people who had phobias. The word 'phobia' comes from the Greek word for unreasonable fear. The people in this documentary used to have normal lives. But now, they stay in their homes all the time. They never go outside their homes because they're afraid of the outside world. So now, they stay inside all the time.

The documentary showed that people would try to help them by going inside to get them and then walking them out real slow. They'd make the phobic person walk out through their front door and down to their entrance gate. Once they reached the gate, they'd turn around and run back to the house. Then their helper would take them out again, this time a little bit further. They'd walk slowly down the street and they'd keep looking back at their house. Some of them would break away from the person trying to help them and they'd run back into the house and shut the door.

The cameras inside the house would film them sweating profusely, just holding the door and shaking. As I watched this, I thought, "This is silly. You ought to just take them out of the house and lock the door!" But that's mean, isn't it? But the thing that amazed me was how this phobia had so dominated them that they'd become a prisoner in their own home.

That's what fear can do. That's what living in the boat, living the 'boat life' can do. Those men in the boat were fishermen. There was no reason for them to be afraid. There'd been storms before. This one was really bad, but it wasn't any worse than others they'd been in. ***But this time, it became serious because of what they did and what they said. They became afraid and they said, "Oh, we're going to perish."***

You've got to watch how you talk, folks. If you're constantly speaking out your worries you'll start believing those negative things you say, you're going to follow the path of your worries.

Now, I'm not trying to make it seem like you've got to be all positive and everything you say has to always be positive. When people see you and say, "Are you sick today?" and you're really sick but you say, "No, I'm not sick" while you obviously are, well, you're sick. ***Well, you don't have to deny that you have symptoms of sickness. You may deny the right of that sickness to be on you, but you don't have to try to be positive to the extent that you deny reality.***

But, the thing is, when fear tells you something to stop you from getting to the other side, don't speak it out, and make up your mind to not believe it. Fear talks. It has a huge vocabulary and it never shuts up. Fear always talks.

What you listen to will affect what you believe…

If you listen to something long enough, you'll start to believe it. This past week, I answered my phone to hear someone ask,

"Is this Mr. Moon?"

I said "Yes, it is."

And they said, "Mr. Moon, we have on our records that you might be interested in refinancing your home."

"Well, not really. I'm not interested."

But this person went on and on and on and on. Now, generally, I say, "I'm not interested, but thank you for calling." And I hang up. This time, I didn't do that.

I stayed on the phone, even though I wasn't interested, and I wasn't really paying attention. The caller went on talking and talking and talking and talking…. and talking. They talked and I listened. Even though I wasn't seriously paying attention, only catching a word here and there, I found myself being sucked in. I began asking questions about refinancing. I don't want to refinance, but the more I listened, the more I began to think, "Well maybe I ought to refinance my house…Yeah, you know…"

Then I caught myself and I thought, "You know what? I need to stop this nonsense. I'm starting to believe this hype. I'm starting to get hooked." That's how fear works. It's always talking to you. When you listen, then you know you're in trouble.

When fear talks and you listen you make yourself vulnerable.

When I was a teenager, I was home by myself watching a scary movie on television. As I was intensely watching the movie, I could've sworn … I saw one of my Mother's dish-towels begin to float across the kitchen! I got so scared I ran out the front door! Then I was embarrassed, because I knew it couldn't be real, but I was so afraid at the time, that my fear made it seem real.

To this day, I remember 'seeing' something floating across the kitchen. But when I went into the kitchen to inspect, all of the dishcloths were where they were supposed to be - none of them had been moved. But the fear was so intense in me that I imagined I'd seen a dish cloth float across the room.

You might be living that kind of life now. You're so afraid, so full of fear, that you're not going to make it, that you're not going to see the glory of God , and not going to be blessed by God that you're negating all the things that God wants to do. You're setting it all aside. You're fooling around in the middle of the sea when God has told you to go over to the other side.

We've got to get out of the 'boat life'. We've got to get out of it. And here's how we do that:

CHAPTER 3
Traveling Protected in God's Promises

*"**No weapon that is formed against thee shall prosper**; and every tongue that shall rise against thee in judgment thou shalt condemn. This is the heritage of the servants of the Lord, and their righteousness is of me," saith the Lord*" (Isaiah 54:17).

We are protected. We are shielded. We are protected by the promise God made in Isaiah 54, amongst other scriptures. These are promises God has made to us, and God doesn't lie. I want you to get this picture.

Imagine that you're driving along in a car. You're protected by the structure of the car. You're on your way to your destination, and as long as you stay in the car, and keep driving along, you'll reach that destination. It's a pretty simple concept: stay in the car and you'll get where you're going, right?

But let's say you open the door while you're driving. You look out and you see that road rushing by. Not real safe, is it? But for whatever reason, you decide to just keep watching that road through the open door. Next thing, you decide to lean your head out of the open door. Then you get really brave and you swing yourself out through the open door, but suddenly, you slip! Boom! You hit the ground and you begin to bounce down the road! Now, I know that's silly and it's also really dumb. You wouldn't do that in real life and maybe it's a bad example, but… I'm using it so that you get my point.

As long as you stay in the car, you're protected. You won't hurt yourself by bouncing down that road and you'll get to your destination. But the minute you swing out of the car, you've removed yourself from that protection and you're going to get hurt. There's going to be a lot of bouncing down the road and a lot of bruises.

You see, this is what the Word of God is saying. In Isaiah it says, *"No weapon formed against thee shall prosper…"*

As long as you stay in faith, and you believe what the scripture says, you're inside the 'car' and you're protected. The doors are closed, the windows are up and nothing gets inside to hurt you, or disturb you because you're protected. But friend, when you begin to doubt the Word of God, when you allow yourself to become afraid, you're opening the doors and you're hanging out. The next thing you know, you've slipped out of the car and you've fallen out and you're bumped up, bruised and disgusted.

Why did this happen? You did not stay inside the promise. Do you understand what I'm saying to you? You've got to stay in the same place as Jesus. If you stay in the boat, the boat is full of fear. The boat is full of all kinds of bad things. The boat is not the place to be. But if you're standing with Jesus on the water, you're in a good place. You're on top of the trouble. You're in a position to get to the other side.

Keep your head in the clouds

Have you heard people saying things like, "Why that young man, or those people, they have their heads in the clouds!" Have you ever heard people saying things like that? Well, you know what? Having your head in the clouds is not a bad thing. If you've got your head in the clouds, you're at least looking up. When people watching you say, "They have always got their heads in the clouds," don't let it bother you.

Let those people stay in the storm if they want. They can stay in the storm getting wet, listening to the thunder and all the rest of the noise the storm's making, while you're looking up, your head in the clouds, enjoying things and not bothered by the storm at all.

It's better to dwell on what's good than on what's wrong. It's better to dwell on the beauty instead of the ugliness. Are you listening to me? It's better to have your mind on something good. Now this is deep. If you'll pay attention, I'm telling you how to get through the storm by walking on the water.

When you're in the worst, find the good! Live and walk in the good. When you're in the worst, quit analyzing the worst, because the worst can only get worse.

But when, in the middle of the storm, you're dwelling on what's good or positive or powerful about a situation, you're in a position to change what's wrong. How many times have you been in the bad times and never got what you wanted while you were focusing on how bad everything was? You've stood in the bad just fussing and complaining and nothing changed.

I was talking to a lady I know the other day. I asked, "How're you doing?"

And she said "Well, I'm doing all right, how about you?"

I answered her saying, "No complaints."

To which she replied, "Well, nobody would listen anyway."

She was right. Nobody wants to hear about your mess. So why do we listen to all the complaints in our own heads when listening won't change a thing? We need to give our problems to God and move on.

Jesus doesn't dwell in trouble, He's a trouble *fixer*!

When you go and tell everybody about your mess, does that make you get out of the mess? No. All you've done is got deeper in the mess and you drew somebody else into the mess with you. And you've got somebody else thinking like you're thinking. The thing is nobody else needs to be there in the bad with you. Get out of the bad. Get out of the boat.

You know what? Jesus doesn't travel in the bad. He can come down and help you get out of the bad, just like He helped Peter. He'll come down into trouble and into pain and He'll pull you out of it. But He doesn't dwell in pain and trouble. He does not. That is not where you'll find Him. By focusing on the bad, it prevents you from connecting with Him.

Some of you are reading this and thinking, "Oooh, when I was at my lowest, Jesus was there."

Well, yes. The Bible says that even in hell you can't hide from God. But it doesn't say He stays in hell. It doesn't say He stays in trouble. He's a trouble fixer! He doesn't stay in it and just hang out with you down there. He wants to pull you out of there.

You've got to move in faith because that's where Jesus moves!

He moves on the water. He's not worrying about getting in the boat with those men. He's not worrying about all that trouble they're going through, because they won't look at him. Am I making you a little nervous because I'm making Jesus seem like He doesn't have any compassion? Don't be. That's not what I'm saying at all.

But what I am saying is that you're not going to see the answers to prayer by staying in unbelief and doubt. *You've got to move in faith because that's where Jesus moves. You've got to move in belief because that's where Jesus moves. You've got to move in the trust of the Lord because that's where He moves.*

You've got to watch what you say if you want to move in faith.

Now if you had someone walking with you that constantly told everybody that you couldn't be trusted, how long would you walk with that person?

Imagine that this person's walking with you, maybe even holding your hand, just walking along with you. As people walk by he's saying to them, "*You know what? You can't trust this person,*" pointing at you. "*This person will get you into trouble.*"

Well pretty soon you'll say, "*Why don't you go somewhere else?*"

"Well, no, I like to walk with you, but I don't trust you. You know what? You're probably leading me somewhere to get me into trouble."

"Well, why don't you leave?" By now, you just want to get rid of this

person.

"Well no. I just like walking with you, but I don't trust you."

How many of you would walk with someone like that? Can you imagine, if everyday you came home, your wife looked at you and said, "*My God, are you home again? What do you want? Did you get paid this week? Well, gimme the money and get outta here."* Anyone who had that kind of marriage would get a divorce. Nobody would stay with somebody like that.

Now, we often act like that, as we walk with the Savior. All the time we're walking with Him, we're talking about all the problems we have and all the troubles we're going through. So often when we're going through trials we talk about how we're not going to make it and how afraid we are. How do you think that makes Him feel when He's given us everything?

Think about it. He died on the cross for us and yet we're still treating Him as if we don't trust Him. Oh folks, the Lord moves in trust and faith, He does not move in defeat. Even when He died on the cross, that wasn't a defeat, it was a victory!

He opened a huge door to usher people through into freedom. He died on the cross to remove the burden of sin so that people could be set free. He broke the power of sin so that people could live in victory instead of defeat. Are you hearing me?

He does not live in that old, negative place, in that bad old place where trouble lives. Now I'm going to prove that to you right now. In Philippians 4:8, Paul's speaking and he says,

"*Finally brethren, whatsoever things are true, whatsoever things are honest, whatsoever things are just, whatsoever things are pure, whatsoever things are lovely, whatsoever things are of a good report. If there be any virtue, any power, any energy, if there be any praise, think on these things*."

He's saying that we need to think about things that are true. Things that are honest, just, pure, lovely and of a good report. Not think about all the bad things that are happening.

Why's he saying that? Because he wants you to move to where Jesus is. When you're where Jesus is, you're where the action is. When you're thinking about good things, because God is good, you position yourself in the realm in which He's moving. You're taking yourself out of the place where the bad things are happening. Where your thoughts are, is where you'll stay. If you want to change your position in life, you have to change how you think.

If you live in fear, if you stay in the boat, and if you continue to hang out with people who live in fear, people who're always crying and always in trouble, you're not going to make it.

When you give up, you die.

I've read many books about concentration camps during World War I I. One of the common denominators I've identified is that most of the people who gave up, died. And most of the ones who wanted to live, who could see a future beyond the gates, and beyond the prison walls, lived.

Many of these books gave examples. One example was a woman who just got up one morning and said, "*I can't deal with this anymore. I just can't deal with this anymore! I'm tired of being in here. I'm tired of the lice in my hair and crawling all over my body. I'm tired of being hungry. I'm tired of just being in this place.*" And she just threw up her hands and said, "*I quit. I give up.*" And within minutes, she died. Just like that.

But then there were others in the same concentration camp who were saying, "*You know what? This day is going to end. I'm going to get out and I'm going to find my family. I'm not going to let this keep me down. There's a life for me. The allies are coming. They're going to liberate us. One day somebody's going to come and open that prison door. And when they open that prison door, I'm going to RUN out of here and I'm going to be free. I remember what it was like to be free. I don't like what I'm going through. I remember in my freedom I was full of joy.*"

They kept their minds picturing being liberated and the life they would have. Those people lived through everything they faced and eventually walked out from behind those prison bars, right through those gates to freedom.

You see, folks, Jesus wants you to think on the things that are going to get you out of your trouble. Stay in your fear and you'll stay in your trouble. Let me say that again: Stay in your fear and you'll stay in your trouble. *Stay in your fear and you will stay in your trouble.*

Doubt and fear keep you chained to the earth and bound to the problem instead of the miraculous solution: When your thoughts are earth bound the Bible says in James 1:6 and 7, "*But when he asks, he must **believe and not doubt**. Because he who doubts is like a wave on the sea, blown and tossed by the wind. **That man should not think he shall receive anything from the Lord.***"

When you're living in doubt, He says, "How do you expect to receive something from me when you're living in doubt?" That's not the place you should be. God doesn't move in the realm of doubt.

CHAPTER 4
Take Yourself Out of the Equation

I know that not everyone is a math major, I'm not either, but I do understand a little bit about math. What I'm going to tell you is simple to understand and it's crucially important. In life you have to take yourself out of the equation.

That's right. You have to take yourself out of the equation. You may say, "What are you talking about?" Let's take a look at the disciples in the boat again. Look at Peter. Peter took himself out of the equation.

Think about it. The boat is pitching, back and forth. It's rolling up and down. Whoosh! The storm is literally destroying the boat. The men in the boat are holding on for dear life. All of a sudden, one of them looks back. "*Oh my gosh! I see a dish rag floating in the air back there!*" No… I'm joking, he said, "*I see a ghost*!"

The 'ghost' is coming closer to the boat, and suddenly, Peter calls out, "*Lord, if it's You…*"

Now remember this, they've been with Jesus for a long time, they'd only recently left him on the other shore. But, because of their fear, they don't recognize him. Jesus is walking on the water. Walks right up to the boat, but still they don't recognize him. They are still blinded by their fear.

Peter, however, says, "Jesus, is that *You*? If it's *You*, bid me come!" He looked beyond the fear and took himself out of the equation. Now they all saw the same thing, but the other disciples didn't see that it was Jesus right next to them. Fear distorts what people see. Fear not only distorts the way people see things, it actually makes *things* look distorted. It makes things look bigger, more threatening, more intimidating and different from what they really are.

The disciples in the boat are crying, "*It's a ghost! It's a ghost! Look, it's a ghost! We're not going to make it!*" That's what fear is telling them. They listen to the fear and that's what they believe. And so that's what they see.

Peter doesn't allow fear to overcome him. So the fear doesn't distort his vision. He sees Jesus. He took himself out of the equation when he got out of that fear-filled boat. In other words, he said, "*I'm not going to stay here with you men. Jesus, if that's You, bid me come.*" Jesus says, "*Come*." Peter acts on Jesus' word. He stepped out on it. He stepped out of the equation.

So what do you do when fear tries to grip you? *Get out of the boat*. You *have* to get out of the boat. You have to *get out of the boat*. You have to step up and say something like this,

"*You know what? I know things are bad and I feel bad and I don't have the money right now,* ***but I'm not going to sit here and worry and be miserable,*** *I'm going to step out of the boat. Jesus, I know you can help me. Bid me come. Help me step out of the boat,*" Then look to Him to bring an answer to your problem. You see, most of us stay in the boat until we're so worn out, crying, "*Oh pleeease...Lord, where are you? God how could you do this?*" We get weaker and weaker the longer we allow ourselves to passively sit in that boat.

No. Instead of just crying about what's wrong, look outside the boat. He's right at the side of the boat. But, if you don't look outside the boat, you won't see Him. If you say, "*How could He leave me like this? I can't understand it. I thought we were friends.*"

He's right there at the side of the boat but you've let the fear blind you and all you're seeing is a ghost. Jesus was right there, but unbelief produced a ghost!

Storm + fear = destruction

Take the fear out of the equation and put Jesus in its place and you have:

Storm + Jesus = a way out

Peter took himself out of the problem, "Bid me come." And Jesus bid him come. He took himself out of the equation.

Now let me make it even simpler. Have you ever been in an argument with someone where you argue and argue and argue? And at some stage during the argument, you suddenly realize that the argument is going nowhere, so you decide to simply stop and walk away.

The people you're arguing with yell, "*Where're you going? Come back here. Don't you hear me talking to you?*"

But you think to yourself, "*It isn't going to make any difference if I stay here and talk to you and let you keep spitting in my face. I can choose to just walk away.*" So you walk away. That's taking your 'self' out of the equation. That's taking yourself out of the unbelief and the trouble and walking away from something that's bad for you, to go to something that's going to help you.

Remember, the disciples were crying and screaming for help, and all the while, Jesus is right by the boat, standing on the water, at the side of the boat, talking to Peter. "*Lord, if that's You, bid me come!*" Jesus answers, "*It's Me...come on.*" In response, Peter steps out of the boat, onto the water.

Now watch this. I've preached this portion of scripture many, many times before I saw what I'm going to share with you now. The Bible says in verses 28 and 29 of Matthew 14, "*Lord, if it's You," Peter said, "Tell me to come to You on the water.*"

"*Come,*" Jesus said. Then Peter got out of the boat and walked on the water and came toward Jesus. Once he stepped out of the boat, *he walked into a miracle*. Once he stepped out of the boat, he walked into a new realm. Once he stepped out of the boat, he walked into something he'd never been in before. He was in a miracle. *He was in a realm where miracles take place*.

Come to Jesus... it's your first resort

Now, I want you to pay attention closely. Jesus said to Peter, "*Come.*" As I studied this, something inside of me kept saying, "Look at the word 'come'. It's important. Look at the word: 'come'." For a while, I kept ignoring the prompt...you know how you do when God's talking to you, but you don't really realize that He is, so you keep ignoring it? So I carried on doing something else. "Look at the word 'come'. You've got to look at that. Look at that word." Finally the Lord got through to me, so I went back and looked at it: "Lord if it's You, bid me *come.*"

In the original Greek, the best translation of the word 'come' is 'resort'. Now can you imagine Jesus standing outside the boat and saying to Peter, "*Resort, Peter.*" I can just hear Peter's puzzled, "*Resort?*" Of course, you know what a resort is. We all know what a resort is. People ask, "*Where are you going?*" and you reply, "I'm *going on vacation.*" "Where to?" "To a resort."

At first the meaning threw me a little bit. So I looked at the word again, and thought, "Wait a minute, wait a minute!" Suddenly I understood. What the word actually means is to find a place of influence, to find a place of establishment. It means: option... alternative. It means remedy. It means *a way out.* The same meaning as when people say, "as a last *resort.*" Jesus is saying to Peter, "*Peter, come to the way out. Peter, come to the remedy. Peter, come to a place where you can kick back and relax and get out of the storm. Come.*"

Wow! When Jesus said, "Come" He meant "Step out of the boat, out of the trouble. Come here and hang out with me, and when you hang out with me you're going to find peace. Resort to Me." When you step out of that old boat, you're going to find peace, but, you've got to step out of that old place you're in. We've got to learn how to think and act differently.

We can't be worrywarts. We can't be complainers. We can't be people who're always seeing what's wrong. We've got to see things from God's perspective. Not from the world's, not from the devil's. We've got to cross over and see things the way God sees them. He's not afraid of the storm. He tells the storm to be quiet. And we're called to be like Him. Whew!

What are you carrying with you through life?

If you're a worrywart, a complainer and you only ever see what's wrong, you'll be weighed down so heavily; you simply won't be able to step out of the boat.

Let me explain what I mean. You know that brides often wear a dress with a long train. I've married brides who've had very long trains. The train is so long that the bride may have already turned the corner but the train will still be following around the corner. Sometimes people will follow the bride and hold the train up off the ground. Have you ever seen that?

And have you ever noticed how happy all those people look? The bride, as well as the people around her who are carrying her train. It's hard to mistake their happiness. In the same way that a bride carries her train with her as she walks down the aisle, so we too all have something that we carry with us as we walk through life. Something that affects us and everyone around us. It's called an 'atmosphere'.

Atmosphere affects everyone nearby.

Have you ever heard people say, "*Golly, when he comes in, the whole room just lights up*"? How many have ever heard that? Certain people have that kind of personality. They walk in and suddenly everyone is happy. As they walk in, people say things like, "*There's Bob!*" And as Bob walks in, cheerful and full of light, everyone around him feels lighter and happier. Everyone wants to hang around him and hear everything he's got to say. There's always a crowd around Bob.

But then there are people with a different kind of personality. The kind of people who, when they walk in, people say things like, "*Oh no, there's Ferguson.*" And they quickly move away. When Ferguson walks in, everyone scatters. Ferguson gets his drink and sits down, but nobody sits by him.Even though there may be no other seats in the room, except those next to Ferguson, nobody sits down because they don't want to sit near him.

We all know people like Bob and Ferguson. The question is which kind of personality are we? The fact is that all of us carry an atmosphere around with us. Our atmosphere is either good or it's bad. ***Our atmosphere is created by how we think about things and how we see things.***

After so many years of dealing with people, I can see by a person's face what kind of atmosphere they're carrying. When I see someone rushing toward me with an angry expression on their face, I know I had better get up and move, because they're mad. That's atmosphere.

Or when people talk to me saying, "PASTOR!" in a really sharp tone, that's atmosphere. All of us have an atmosphere that we carry with us and that other people can feel as soon as they are close to us, see us or talk to us. Our atmosphere affects how people respond to us.

As a kid, I learned early about atmospheres. We used to play all day long at my house, when I was a kid. And my Mom…I'd just love you to meet my Mom; she's just so different, so special. But we'd play, and my Mom would laugh. Sometimes she'd tease with us and chase us through the house. We just had great times with my Mom. It was a really happy, fun atmosphere.

But, every day, just before six o'clock, everything in the house began to simmer down. The volume in the house became lower and lower until it was really quiet. At six o'clock, we'd look out the window and we'd see my Dad's black truck drive up.

Brrr. Brrr. Boom! Stop. And out of the truck would emerge my Dad. He's dirty. He's been under cars all day. We'd watch him walking toward the door. He'd be carrying a black lunch pail. He always came through the back door because Mom would make him take his clothes off before he got into the house. He'd open the door. Us kids would stand at the back door and look at him with big eyes. He'd open the screen… CREAK…

"Hi Dad!" you'd hear our high pitched kid voices cry. He wouldn't say anything. Just grunt and walk in… The rest of the night, everybody in the house was quiet.

Oh, how I used to hate it when my Mom would say, "Lonzo, help Norman with his homework!" I'd groan inside, "Oh no….", because he'd sit down with me and I could just feel his atmosphere saying, "*Why don't you understand this!?*" Sometimes, he'd get so mad at me, he'd get up and slam the chair against the table and leave so that he wouldn't hit me. He had *atmosphere*.

But, I'm happy to say, down the road, many years later, my Dad met Jesus! It was one of the biggest testimonies in our city. People who had known him previously, knew there'd been a miracle, after he'd accepted Jesus, because he was different. The Lord changed him. Changed his atmosphere. Changed who he was.

That's why you'll see Paul saying so often in the Bible, "Die to the flesh." That's why the Bible is full of "Let this mind be in you that was also in Christ Jesus." That's why the Bible talks about killing the 'old man' in your life, or that old nature in your life. That's why it's full of that.

Jesus wants to enable you to change that old, bad atmosphere. He wants you to come out of that 'Loserville' that you've been living in and really live in victory. And He's saying to us today, "*You CAN be changed! You CAN be different. You don't have to be the way you've been all these years. You CAN be free!*"

You can choose which way you travel:

Today is the day it can happen. There are two ways to travel. You can travel in fear. You can travel in the boat and be held in fear by those tentacles. You can travel in that place of defeat where you see only the 'ghosts'…or, you can travel with Jesus, on top of the water, on top of the troubles, positioned with Jesus to take authority over the storm instead of being destroyed by it.

It's your choice. It's a choice you can make today. If you want to see Jesus, instead of the 'ghost', you have to trust Him. **He won't let you drown in the storm if you call out to Him. He's standing right there, at the side of your boat and He's holding out His hand to you.**

Maybe you already know Jesus. Like those disciples who'd walked with Him and thought they knew Him well – but they found when the storm hit, that they forgot all about who He was. They couldn't see Him anymore. All they could think about and see was a distorted picture created by their fear. They listened to the storm that lied to them, saying, "*You're not going to make it,*" and they forgot that Jesus had told them to go over to the other side.

Maybe you've been listening to the storm, believing the lies that the devil has been telling you. If you have, take heart. It's not too late to choose to see Jesus. Understand that the Bible says that the devil is a liar. He's the father of ALL lies. So if he's telling you something, you can be guaranteed, it's a lie.

Fear comes from the devil, so if you've been fearful, you know that Jesus came to set you free from fear. The Bible says in Romans 8:32, "*He that spareth not His own Son, but delivered him up for us all, how shall He not with Him also freely give us all things?"*

And, in Matthew 7:7 it says, "*Ask, and it shall be given you; seek and ye shall find; knock and it shall be opened unto you."*

The thing is we all have situations where we need help. The Bible says that God wants to help us. But the devil wants to stop us asking for, and believing for, and then getting the help we need.

You might say, "*But God is so powerful. If He wants to help, how can the devil stop Him?*" That's a good question. The devil can't stop God, but you can. "*What do you mean!?*"

The devil can delay the answer to your problems and that's where your faith comes in. If you asked God for something and it fell right in your lap that second, you wouldn't need to have faith. The devil figures if he can make you think that God hasn't heard your prayer, or doesn't care, or isn't able to do anything to help you, then you'll stop calling on Him and you'll give up.

If you ask God for help and then keep worrying about whether He's going to help you or not, the Bible calls that 'doubt'. Now doubt's a very dangerous thing and it's about the only thing that can stop God from helping you.

The Wikipedia dictionary says this about doubt:'Doubt – *uncertainty in the context of trust (where it takes the form of distrust), action, decision or belief. It implies challenging some notion of reality in effect, and may involve hesitating to take a relevant action due to concern that one might be mistaken or at fault. The term 'to doubt' can also mean to question one's circumstances and life experience.*

Doubt will knock you out.

When you ask God for help and you don't see it arrive right away, you've got to keep holding on, trusting that He will help you. Time can be the biggest challenge we face when we are stepping out of the boat.

We call to Jesus. He gives us a word. We step out on it, but we don't see the answer right away. Sometimes we're out there standing on the water and we find that it's really hard to keep standing on that word when the waves are crashing around us and the wind is howling in our face.

But this is what James 1:1-8 tells us:

> *"Consider it a sheer gift, friends, when tests and challenges come at you from all sides. You know that* ***under pressure, your faith-life is forced into the open and shows its true colors****.*
>
> *So don't try to get out of anything prematurely. Let it do its work* ***so you become mature and well-developed, not deficient in any way. If you don't know what you're doing, pray to the Father.***
>
> ***He loves to help. You'll get his help, and won't be condescended to when you ask for it. Ask boldly, believingly, without a second thought. People who "worry their prayers" are like wind-whipped waves. Don't think you're going to get anything from the Master that way, adrift at sea, keeping all your options open."***
> (The Message)

Did you see that? James says, "*If you don't know what you're doing, pray to the Father. He loves to help.*" You don't have to beg God. You just have to go to Him and ask. He wants to help! He's waiting for you to ask Him so that He can help.

James says, "*Ask boldly, believingly, without a second thought.*" When we do this it's proof that we really do trust Him, just like a child in a stable home trusts their parents to look after them.

What stops God from helping us, more often than not, is when we 'worry our prayer.' When we keep worrying that He won't answer, or hasn't heard us, or that it'll be too late, then really, what we're saying is, "*God, I don't really believe you're going to come through for me. I'm not sure I can trust you on this one. Maybe I'd better look for help somewhere else.*" And the

Bible says that when we do that, we don't get anything.

That's why the Bible tells us that we have to develop endurance. What does it mean to have endurance? Well, the dictionary says that 'endurance' means '*the ability to withstand hardship or adversity; especially the ability to sustain a prolonged stressful effort or activity'*.

Think about the endurance a marathon runner has to have if they're going to complete their race. Even when their muscles are screaming in pain, when their mind tells them to give up, end the pain and relax, they don't quit. Why don't they quit? Because; they want to reach the finish line. The prize. That's where they're headed. That's their destination. That's where they're going and they're not going to quit until they get there.

It's the same way when we're in the storm. We need to develop endurance. If we forget about where we're going and just sit in the middle of the sea crying… if we give in when the going gets tough, we'll never get to our destination. If we stay in the boat, we'll likely sink. But if we call out to Jesus and step out onto the water, onto His word, and keep believing He'll not let us down…we'll make it. We'll be able to walk on top of that trouble and tell the storm to be still. We'll be able to walk on top of that trouble, right over to the other side.

Someone once said: "*However, some people are so foolish that they stop everything whenever they have a doubt. The momentum of their hearts and minds, the tremendous forward movement of their target, is stopped dead while they fumble around with a limited mind, seeking in a generally half-hearted way for some powerful answer. Even if they received a powerful answer, chances are these hopefuls would not understand such an answer, being unequipped as yet in terms of concepts and in terms of mental/emotional maturity to appreciate it.*"

We can't afford to stay in the boat doing nothing but worrying about the 'ghosts'. We have to see Jesus. We have to step out of that boat and onto the water. If you're stuck in that boat today, you can decide right now to get out. You can decide right now that you're not going to let that storm walk on top of you any longer. You're not going to let the fear blind you. You're going to see Jesus.

If you've never met Jesus personally:

If you've never met Jesus personally, you can do that right now. Without Him, you'll never be able to step out of the boat. Imagine if Peter had tried to step out of the boat all on his own, without Jesus. He'd have sunk right away. None of us has what it takes to walk on water without Jesus. None of us can save ourselves. The good news is that none of us has to. God has made a way for us. We can ask Jesus to save us right now.

What do I mean by 'save us'?

Salvation is a state of having 'eternal life'. It's being in a right relationship with God. It's becoming His child. Without Jesus in our hearts, we cannot have this. The Bible says that, "*God so loved the world that He sent His only begotten Son that whosoever believes in Him should not perish, but have eternal life*" (John 3:16).

Anyone can be saved no matter what they have done.

In Romans 3 it says, "*...the righteousness of God which comes by believing with personal trust and confident reliance on Jesus Christ. It is meant for all who believe...Since all have sinned and are falling short of the honor and glory which God bestows and received. All are justified and made upright and in right standing with God, freely and gratuitously by His grace (His unmerited favor and mercy), through the redemption which is provided in Jesus Christ, Whom God put forward before the eyes of all as a mercy seat and propitiation by His blood (the cleansing and life-giving sacrifice of atonement and reconciliation, to be received) through faith....*" (Romans 3:22-25 (Amplified Bible).

All you have to do is...

1. **Accept** – that God loves you, that Jesus died for you so that your sins (past, present and future) are now paid for and God's gift to you is a brand new life in Him as His child. If you
2. **Believe** that Jesus is the Son of God who came to earth to live in the flesh as a man and be crucified and then raised from the dead,

3. **Confess** – which means to say out loud to others that Jesus is Lord and that He died and rose from the dead (Acts 16:31; Romans 10:9-10).

If you would like to accept this gift and you believe with all your heart and you confess this with your mouth, then the Bible says that you are saved! All you need to do is tell God that you accept His gift of salvation. Don't worry if you're not used to praying. Praying is just talking to God the way you would talk to your best friend. Here's an example of how you can pray and ask Jesus to be your Lord and Savior.

> "*Dear Father,*
>
> *I accept the gift of eternal life that You have given me. I believe that Jesus is the Son of God Who came to earth to live as a Man in the flesh. I believe that He died for me and was buried, but on the third day, You raised Him from the dead. I believe that Jesus is Lord.*
>
> *Please, Jesus come into my heart and be Lord over my life. I give my life to You and ask You to lead me and guide me from now on.*
>
> *Thank You for saving me, making me into a new creation and making me Your child. I receive this gift by faith and I understand that I can't work to earn it or be good enough to deserve it on my own, but that You give it to me because You love me as much as You love Jesus* (John 17:23). *From now on, I am yours.*"

If you just prayed that prayer, then congratulations! You are now saved. The next thing you should do is tell someone – that's part of confessing with your mouth.

To help you learn more about life with God, you should find and regularly attend a Bible believing church and read your Bible every day. If you'd like help finding a church in your area, you may contact us by email at rolchuch@aol.com

PART TWO
Do You See Jesus?

"It couldn't have been more awkward. I was in the middle of cleaning house and still had to bake, when He arrived. He smiled and greeted me so lovingly, I was tempted to drop everything and just be with Him. Instead, I left Him to sit while I prepared a meal. Thank God, Lazarus had just slaughtered a goat! I'd make a stew. While it simmered, I'd bake. Oh... and I would need to get some vegetables picked and prepared. And...oh, my goodness! There was no clean linen. Not even a clean cloth to set before Him! And while they waited, I should be offering them fresh bread with cheese and wine. Only there was no fresh bread. What would He think!? Anxiety and embarrassment flooded my heart.

Where was Mary! Drat that girl! Head in the clouds again. She should be here helping me. Instead, she's just sitting at His feet, relaxing! I ask you! Has she no consideration? Don't they care? Why doesn't He send her to help? It's not fair.

Does He expect me to do this all by myself! I pounded the dough angrily. What'd happen if I just sat there, as well? Would they get anything to eat? No... Then what!? Misery welled up inside like red hot bile.

Finally, I could stand it no longer.

I strode in before Him, hands on my hips and fire in my eyes. He stopped talking Everyone turned to look at me, including wide-eyed, innocent looking Mary...

He smiled, waiting for me to speak. I swallowed nervously, then thought of myself working frantically to serve them and the anger returned. My voice came out harsher than I intended, "Lord, is it nothing to you that my sister has left me to serve alone?"

I couldn't look into His eyes. I focused on his chin instead. I turned my anger on Mary, whose fault it really was... "Tell her then to help me. Tell her to lend a hand and do her part along with me!" I could hear my strident tone fade to a whimper as self-pity overwhelmed me.

He took my hands in His large, calloused hands and I felt His warmth flowing over me. For a second, He was silent, then, forcing me to look Him in the eyes, He said softly, "Martha. Martha," and sighed. "You are anxious and troubled about many things. There is need of only one thing. Mary has chosen the good portion. The portion that is to her advantage. It shall not be taken away from her."

His love, His power flowed into me. For the first time, I understood. He was right. None of the things that drove me really mattered. They'd make no difference a month from now a week from now... even a day from now. Jesus was here. He was here now. Soon, He'd be gone. Why should I waste my time fretting about food and linen? When they were hungry, we would eat. He would take care of everything."

CHAPTER 5
Jesus is in the House

I want to ask you a question. Do you see Jesus? That may seem like a strange question, but think about it while we look at a story about Mary and Martha found in Luke 10:38-42.

The Bible says, *And it came to pass as He went that He entered into a certain village and a certain woman named Martha received Him into her house. And she had a sister called Mary which also sat at Jesus' feet and heard His Word. But Martha was cumbered with much serving and came to Him and said, "Lord, does Thou not care that my sister hath left me to serve alone? Bid her therefore that she help me" And Jesus answered and said unto her, "Martha. Martha. Thou art careful and troubled about many things, but one thing is needful, and Mary has chosen that good part and it shall not be taken away from her."*

If you ask Jesus into the house, don't forget that He's there...

The thing is, many of us have received Jesus into the house. Many of us have asked the Lord to come into our lives. We've asked him to come in and save us and we've been so thankful that he's done so, and it's made a huge difference to our lives.

But the problem is, just like Martha, many of us don't actually *see* Jesus anymore. **We don't see Him.**

The reason is, that just like Martha, so many things in this world, and in our lives, have overcome us. We're so interested in foolish things; we're so caught up in areas of life that really aren't important.

One day, every one of us is going to die. Now, I know some of you *think* you're never going to die. Some of you *think* you're going to live forever. Especially young people. Young people think they're just going to live forever.

I understand this because I was young once too and thought I would never get old. Now, as I'm writing this, I'm not young anymore. And I'm saying to myself, "Hey! What happened here?"

Jokes aside, the truth is that we tend to get caught up in things that we think are so very important at the time. But, when we stand before God, it's not going to be about what kind of car you drove, or what kind of house you lived in. It won't be about how you did this, or how you did that, or how good or bad you were at a certain thing.

It's not going to be about all those things we thought were so important. What's going to count is: did you see Jesus? Did you see Jesus in your life? When you were struggling with life, going through trials, did you *see* Jesus?

When people came to you for help, did you see Jesus? Did you take time to see Jesus? When you really *see* Jesus, you know that everything's going to be all right. Everything's going to be all right because Jesus is the answer to every situation.

Now I've shared many times about how I've been at the bedsides of people who are passing away. Going from that hospital bed into eternity. And I've seen some of them so full of joy because they were ready to go. But, I've also been with some that have been really apprehensive. They were afraid to let go of life, because they weren't sure about where they were going. What was the difference? Those that were excited were seeing something that others could not see. They were seeing Jesus.

The cares of life will blind you to the blessings of life, if you let them. The Bible says that Martha was 'cumbered down'. In other words, she was so weighed down with things she thought were important, that she didn't realize what she had.

So many of us don't understand how blessed we are, *when* we're blessed. Now did you see that? Some of us don't understand how blessed we are until that blessing is taken away from us, or something bad happens to us, and all of a sudden we realize the value of the blessing that we had.

Every one of us has been blessed. We've been blessed because God has blessed us. Every good thing we have, or has happened to us, in life is a blessing, and all good things come from God. But, more often than not, we don't appreciate those blessings.In this Bible story, Martha is busy running around the house doing what people do during the holidays. She's fixing food. She's running back and forth.

Her whole reason for being mad is that her sister, Mary, doesn't want to move from where she's sitting to help her. Why? Why doesn't Mary want to move? Because, Mary sees Jesus. Mary *sees* Jesus. Mary is sitting at His feet and experiencing the greatest peace she's ever known in her life.

But, Martha's running around. Martha doesn't see the blessing she has, right there in her home. Martha doesn't realize how blessed she really is, because she's too busy with other things. Now I ask you, how often are you so busy and caught up in other things that you're not seeing Jesus?

Many of us are going through situations and through problems. Although He's with us, accessible to us, we're seeing the problems, we're not seeing Jesus. Many of us are struggling with *things* and so the struggle gets harder and harder, because we're not seeing Jesus. While we're seeing the struggle instead of seeing Jesus, things just get tougher and tougher.

When the Bible uses the word 'cumbered' it means that she was weighed down and driven mentally. It means that she was too busy with other things to connect with the Lord of Glory, the Lord of Heaven. How critical it is to not be so busy that you miss God. You know it can happen. You can be so busy that you miss God. Martha thinks that fixing a meal for all these people is a whole lot more important than dealing with the very Man who's about to raise her brother from the dead.

Now, I'm going to tell you something. When her brother had died and was in that grave, the thought in Martha's mind was, "*Where was Jesus? Where was Jesus when I needed Him? Where was He when I needed to call Him? When I needed Him to do something I couldn't do? Where was Jesus?*"Then, at that time, I bet that her mind went back to this very moment, when she was so busy cooking, that she was too busy for Jesus. Again, I have to ask you: *do you see Jesus*?

Being overly concerned about the impression you're making is a key distraction.

The Bible says Martha was *careful* about many things. Her mind was constantly running. Not only does 'careful' mean that she was running back and forth fixing a meal and thinking about all she had to do, but it also means that Martha was promoting her own interests.

In other words, Martha wanted to cook this big meal, so that, later, she could sit amongst all the people who were eating, and hear them say: "*Oh Martha, Martha, how did you come up with this*? -- *Oh Martha, the gravy is so creamy.* -- *Oh Martha, there's never been a cook like you, Martha*! -- *Oh Martha! Martha would you come over to my house and show me how to do this*?"

Some of us have that same problem. We want people to notice who we are, all the time. I always have a problem with loud people. I have relatives that are loud. The minute they come into a place, you know that they're there. You hear them say things like, "*Hey, yeah! And you know what I told 'em*?" at the top of their voices. When I hear them, I want to say, "Will you stop? Will you *stop*!"

They do it because they want to be noticed. **The thing is, whenever we promote our needs, or our interests, making them more important than knowing God, I want to tell you: you're going to get your wish. You're going to get the very thing you want.** Your interests *are* going to be way above God's – *but, you're going to miss God when you need him to come through for you.*

When He comes by, at the time when you need Him the most, you're not going to be there, in a position to receive from Him, because you're in a different place: you're somewhere else, promoting your interests.

And because you're not where He is, you'll miss Him. You're not where He is, because you're so busy trying to promote who you are as a person, that you simply don't see Him. You're so busy trying to promote your interests that you forget all about Him.

When tests come, if you're not already seeing Jesus, you'll probably fail.

Recently, I had a dream. I dreamed that I was in California with some trusted Christian friends of mine. In this dream, they were renting a building. There was also a sinister character in the dream. This person came to me and said, "*You know that your friends are renting this building. But did you know, we're 'scratching each other's backs'?*"

I remember hearing that. And I thought, "*Scratching each other's backs*? What are you talking about?"

He continued, "You know what? Your friends are doing really good things in public, where everyone can see, but behind the scenes, we're all doing something really corrupt. But, we have an agreement: they're not telling anyone about us and we're not telling anyone about them, either."

Now, please, remember this: if you ever see my good friends, don't ever tell them I said they were doing crooked things. Far from it! This story has no basis in reality, it is just a dream! But, even though it was just a dream, I thought, "*How do I respond to this? Do I get sucked into this, or do I stand up and say, 'Well I'm sorry, but, whether they do this or not, I'm not going be involved.'*"

Did you know that even in dreams, you are sometimes tested? I can remember in this dream, the sinister character trying to get me to side with evil, saying to me, "*Come on... come over to our side and do what we do.*"

I remember responding, "*No, buddy, I can't do that because I serve Jesus Christ. He's my personal Savior and I can't go the way you're going.*" When I woke up, I woke up with a smile on my face, because I knew that I had passed that test.

I knew that things were right in my life and I knew that for me, the most important thing is to have Him. He says that if we have Him, then we'll have everything else we'll ever need as well.

He said that if we seek Him first, if we come and look to Him, and want Him first, before everything else that we want, that He will make sure that everything else comes to us.

Seek ye first the Kingdom of God and all these things shall be added

unto you. A lot of people are missing that provision because they're trying to promote themselves and get the things they want, instead of getting Jesus who has *everything* you want. Hallelujah!

Remember Martha? Martha is trying to promote her own interests. She's looking for her self-worth from the reactions of the people she's trying to impress, instead of getting it from Jesus. The Bible says she was troubled. Jesus said to her, "*Martha, Martha thou are careful and troubled about many things.*"

When He uses that term 'troubled', He meant that her head was crowded. Or, to put it in even simpler terms, He meant that there was a 'crowd' in her head. Now what does that mean? People who know me, know that I always hear a lot of things in my head. A lot of people do. Martha was someone who had a lot going on in her head. These 'voices' kept distracting her from what was really important. So many of us are in that same boat today.

Be aware of what's going on inside your head – the devil will keep you busy thinking about yourself simply to distract you from seeing Jesus.

Stop for just a moment. Think about what's going on inside your head most of the time. Chances are there are a lot of things running through your mind all the time.

Many times, these things are worries. The reason this happens is that the devil wants you to miss what Jesus is saying. He is using these thoughts, or voices, to distract you.

That's one of the ways he operates. He always does this when he wants you to miss something important that's being said. When you realize that your mind is racing a mile a minute, it's a good idea to simply stop; clear your head of all the distractions, take a breath, and listen for what Jesus is trying to tell you.

Have you ever noticed how often you'll be watching a television program and the phone will ring just as the story is coming to a climax? Has that ever happened to you? Happens to me all the time! I'll be watching the program and just as I'm about to find out who the murderer was and what actually happened – just as all the answers are about to be revealed and I'm on the edge of my seat… the phone will ring. Somebody calls and asks if I want to put siding on my house. It's frustrating!

That's the way the devil works. The devil wants you to miss what's important. And when the Lord is moving and speaking to you, the devil will immediately come and begin to crowd your head with all kinds of distractions. He begins to speak things to you and put thoughts in your mind to distract you away from Jesus.

When I studied this story about Martha and Mary having Jesus in their house, I realized that this was a typical example of how the devil will attempt to distract us, if we let him. Here Mary sits down and can't tear herself away from Him.

Martha's busy in another part of the house, complaining, like most of us do, saying, "*Lord, don't you care what's happening to me? Don't you care, God, that I've been working so hard? Don't you care God that I'm here by myself and nobody is helping me?*"

Sound familiar? "*God, come on, what about me*?"

Well honey, if you'd just stop what you're doing and come on over to where Jesus is and sit down at His feet, you'd get the help you need. Those distractions would just fade away into the 'nothing' they really are and you'd be free to receive from Jesus.

Now, that brings me back to my original question: do *you* see Jesus? Do you *see* Jesus? **When trouble comes, seeing Jesus is the only safe place to be.** I believe that the day is coming where we're going to really need to see Jesus. Recently, I was studying some scriptures that speak about the end times and relating them to how events are coming together in the world today.

The things that are going on in the Middle East right now are so clearly described in scripture, that it's hard for anyone to dismiss what the Bible says. The Bible called all these things long before any of them happened. It says that one day, the nations are going to gather in the valley of Meggido and they're going to fight. During this war, the blood is going to rise to the height of a horse's rein because so many people are killed. **I have to say again, there is coming a day when we're going to have to know Jesus a whole lot better than we know Him now.** We're going to have to depend on Him a whole lot more than we depend upon Him now.

Think about it. What are you going to do when, one day, you turn on the water in your house and the water doesn't run? What're you going to do about that? What're you going to do when you can't just call on the phone and order water to come to your house?

As you probably know, there are people living in that state right now. People who don't have water. And right now, water is more important to them than anything else in the world, but they don't have it.

Well, the day's coming when we're not going to have the plenty that we're experiencing now – life is going to get tough and without faith, it's going to be even tougher.

If you don't know Jesus and you can't *see* Him, life is going to get a whole lot tougher than it is right now. When a loved one is lying on their deathbed long before their time and you don't *see* Jesus, you're going to lose people that are precious to you.

You have to make sure you're in a position to receive His help. Don't allow yourself to be distracted by the 'crowd' in your head. Practice it now so that when you're under pressure, you're already used to seeing Jesus and looking to Him for the answer.

There was a lady named Mary Woodworth-Etter who had a healing ministry in the late 1800's. She lost six of her family before she finally grasped that God was a healer. Six people in her family had died, almost randomly. She talked about how she lay at their beds and prayed and asked God, "*Where are you? Why aren't you hearing me? God why aren't you making a difference*?"

But then she began to see Jesus. She began to lay hold of Him and to get really serious about serving Him, looking to Him, trusting Him and walking with Him like she never had before.

After a while, when she began to pray for her loved ones as well as other sick people, they started getting healed. They started getting up off sick beds, off deathbeds, because God was now able to minister through this woman's life.

'Playing church' will soon be a thing of the past.

There's coming a time when it's not going to be enough to just come to church. There's coming a time when it's not going to be enough to just say, "Oh yes, I'm a Christian." You're going to be tried by the very words that you're speaking.

I get a paper every month from a ministry that works in communist countries such as China, as well as in Mexico and South America. They minister in places that are hostile to the Gospel. In this paper, I've read testimonies of people who have been shot because they believe in Jesus. Others have been thrown out of their homes.

I've read stories about Muslims whose parents disowned them when they received Jesus. Imagine throwing your child out of your home and deciding to never know them again because they became a Christian!

I heard a powerful testimony when I attended a conference at the Adam's Mark Hotel about a year and a half ago. A young man described how they were pulled off a bus in South America. They were all lined up in a ditch and one by one, the bandits shot these people in the back of the head.

They shot the man who was testifying in the back of the head as well, but he didn't die. As he recovered, God sent him to the very person that had shot him and he led that man to the Lord. I'm telling you, 'playing church' is going to soon be a thing of the past.

When the fire of persecution really hits, not everybody's going to be prepared to withstand it. Don't get mad at me now. Don't be upset with me. It's a fact: if you're not really serious about Jesus, you're not going to last when you're under attack.

When I preach messages like that, I can almost hear people saying, "Oh, Pastor, don't say things like that. You know Pastor, we almost filled up all the chairs today, Pastor, don't say things like that."

Unfortunately, I have to say things like that because they're true. If you're not serious and paying attention to the Master, if you're not serious about serving God, you're not going to make it. Christianity is not what you do in your spare time. It's what you'd better be doing all the time.

Jesus is not a part time love. Do you remember that old blues song that says, "I'm gonna find me.... Do duh doo... a part time... luuuv...?"

No, you don't need a part time love, you need a real love. One that's going to stand with you; through thick and thin. I ask you again, do you see

Jesus? Do you see Jesus?

CHAPTER 6

The Day Jesus Stood Up

The other day, I was reading the story about the stoning of Stephen, which is found in the New Testament. In this story, the religious people of the day are stoning this poor boy.

The Bible says that Saul, who later became Paul, the apostle, is standing by, watching, holding the coats of the others as they're stoning this young man. Picture it… they're throwing rocks at Stephen. They're slinging rocks and stones just as hard as they can and these missiles are hitting this boy's body. If you read the story, you'll find that this young man, even as the rocks are being thrown at him, says, "*I see Jesus standing next to the Father*" (Acts 7:55).

Note what he says: "*I see Jesus standing next to the Father.*" If you read the scriptures carefully, you'll see that he doesn't see Jesus sitting next to the Father, he sees Jesus *standing* next to the Father. Jesus is standing up, looking at this man who's being stoned to death and hailing him, cheering him on because he's holding fast to what he believes. While this is happening, Jesus is strengthening Stephen to continue to hold fast to his faith, even though he's suffering intense persecution.

When I read that, I said, "Oh my God! God, Himself, actually got up off the throne and came and looked down to earth and said 'Look at that boy, that's one of mine!' "

Right after Stephen says that he saw Jesus next to the Father, it says in Acts 7:60 that, "*he kneeled down, and cried with a loud voice, "Lord, lay not this sin to their charge." And when he had said this, he fell asleep.*"

Oh friend, when you're able to do that in the midst of a severe trial, you've been in touch with somebody greater than yourself. When we're going through trouble, that's what we need: to be in touch with Jesus.

As Stephen took this punishment, he was seeing Jesus and it empowered him to rise above everything that was happening and even forgive his tormentors. In doing this, he gave us a pattern. He showed us that when you really see Jesus, you get past the pain and you're empowered.

One day you'll have a problem where you're going to have to ask for help.

Be honest, can you fix all your problems? Oh we may think we can… but, I want to tell you, you can't fix everything. One day you'll have a problem that will be too difficult and you're going to have to call out and say "Help me!"

When my wife went through surgery, she told me that the thing that was worse for her than all of the surgery, the pain, the incision, or anything else, was that she couldn't do anything for herself. They operated on Debbie, and then used huge, big staples to close her up. I felt so bad because I couldn't help her. I was there with her, but there was nothing I could do to ease the pain.

She said "*Honey if it hadn't been for you and my mother and the kids, I couldn't have survived.*" She told me, "*It made me appreciate what I've got, so much more.*"

When you're going through a time when you can't do anything to help yourself, you need Jesus.

As you might've guessed, I love to read, and I read a lot. Once I read about a lady who arrived home one day to find that her husband was gone. She said that she walked into the house and didn't see him, so she began looking for him. She saw that her kids were all there. She went into their bedroom and found that his clothes were gone. Everything was gone. She looked in the garage, and his car was gone.

She was terrified, remembering that he'd always been fussing at her because she had gained weight. He kept telling her, "*I'm leaving you because I can't stand it.*" And, then, he left her. I'm glad everybody with an overweight spouse doesn't leave home.

Anyway, in the story, the lady stated: "*I sat there for three days and cried. For three days I did nothing but cry. I just wept because I didn't know what to do and I kept saying to myself, 'What am I going to do? What am I going to do? He's gone. The money's gone. What are the kids going to do? How could he do that?'*"

For three days she went over the situation again and again and again. Then on the third day, something happened to her. She heard something say, "*You can't sit here forever. What are we going to do? Just quit living? You have kids to raise, you've got a life to live.*"

She said that suddenly, something began to strengthen inside her, and she heard herself saying, "Well, he's gone. Well, we've got to do something about that."

You know what she did? She got up from there. She went back to school and began raising her kids. This abandoned wife and mother went back to school and raised her kids *on her own*. Not only that, but, in the process, she also lost a substantial amount of weight. She lost so much weight that the husband started coming back around again.

Now she was a good girl...and you may think I'm going to say she forgave him. No... she just showed him the hand, and said, "Baby, you *wish* you had all this...but you were married to the fat lady, remember?"

Step into a victorious realm by focusing on Jesus.

When I read that story, it made me think. There are times when we are pressed into a place where we *have* to find Jesus, where we have to see Him; because there's no alternative...we can't get out of where we are *unless* we can tap into Jesus, unless we can take hold of His life, unless we can look to Him.

Stephen was seeing Jesus so clearly, that even though the crowd was throwing stones at his head, he didn't experience the pain, because he was focusing so intensely on Jesus. He saw the Lord of Lords and King of Kings and he wasn't worried about what's going on anywhere else because he saw the power of glory. What was happening physically had no power over him. He had stepped into a different realm.

And then, to top it all, while they were killing him, they heard him ask the Father to forgive them. You can't do that unless you see Jesus. Remember where in Acts 7:60 it says, "(Stephen) fell asleep"? To me that means that Stephen died once he had readied himself to make the transition to the Lord. He was so focused on the Master he checked out of this world on his own terms!

CHAPTER 7
God Will Even Use An Ass

One of my favorite stories is about Balaam. If you're not sure who Balaam is, you can read about him in the Old Testament in Numbers 22 to 24. Balaam was a prophet. The story I'm referring to is about Balaam and the ass. Balaam was a prophet, but that didn't mean that he was all that spiritual. Just because you're a preacher, it doesn't make you really spiritual!

You may be surprised that I'd say that, seeing as I'm a preacher. I say it because it's true. Just because somebody gets up in front of people doesn't make them spiritual.

Balaam was an Old Testament prophet, who would see things. In other words, he had visions and claimed to talk to God. But Balaam had a problem. Balaam was locked into a bad relationship. He was in love with mammon. He was in love with money. One day, Balak, the son of the King of Moab, came to Balaam and wanted to hire him to curse the children of Israel.

God tells Balaam "I *don't want you fooling with these people*." He said, "*There's no way in the world I'm going to let you curse these people because they're blessed. You're not going to curse them. Every curse you throw against them I will cause blessing to come on them.*"

Balaam's Boo Boo – ignore God at your own risk

The Bible says that one day Balaam saddles up his ass and goes to join Balak, even though he realized that God didn't want him to try to curse the Israelites. On his way to join Balak, the Angel of the Lord blocked his way three times. **Now, Balaam couldn't see the Angel of the Lord, but his ass did**. The Angel of the Lord blocked his way because he was going somewhere that God didn't want him to go. He was going to a join a group of people that wanted him to curse Israel whom God had blessed.

As he's riding his donkey to join Balak, the Bible says, the Angel of the Lord stood in his way holding a fiery sword. The donkey immediately saw the Angel of the Lord and stopped. Balaam got mad and beat the donkey. Balaam tried hard to push the donkey forward. Reluctantly, the donkey began to move forward a little, but then it went off to the side, into a field.

Balaam cursed and beat his donkey again. He was so mad that he was just tearing this donkey up.

The donkey again moved a little bit further, but again, suddenly stopped. By now Balaam and the donkey are between two rock walls. The donkey saw the Angel of the Lord again and the poor animal just shut down. He did not want to take on the Angel with his fiery sword! The donkey moved over, close against the wall crushing Balaam's foot. Balaam became so mad with the donkey that he began to beat him with his staff.

The Bible says that God then gave the donkey power to talk. Now, I don't know about you, but sometimes when I read these stories, I ask myself, '*What kind of fools are these people?*'

What does God have to do to get *our* attention?

If a donkey started to talk to me it would get my attention in a hurry. If I'm standing there and all of a sudden a donkey starts going "Uh.. well, hello…my name is George…" You know what? I would probably hardly be able to speak. I'd probably just gasp, "What!?"

But here is Balaam's donkey asking Balaam, '*Why are you beating on me? Haven't I been faithful to you from the beginning?*" And, by all accounts, Balaam doesn't even act surprised that his donkey is talking to him!

Instead, he's so mad with the donkey that he answers – just as if he and the donkey were in the habit of having a conversation every day! He says to the donkey, "*I beat you and if I had a sword I would've stabbed you and killed you.*" All of a sudden, Balaam looks up and sees the Angel of the Lord. He gets scared and says, "*I didn't know*!"

In Numbers 22:34 it says, *"And Balaam said to the Angel of the Lord, "I have sinned for I knew not that thou stoodeth in the way against me. Now therefore if it displease thee I will get me back again."*

You will only see God when you really, truly want to.

I believe that there are people who have gotten themselves killed because they couldn't see the Angel of the Lord. I believe that there are people who have lost their lives before their time because they could not see what God was doing and where God was going.

I believe that there are people who have missed out on eternity because they could not see what God was trying to accomplish and what He was doing. They move in a direction that God does not want them to go. If they could only see!

CHAPTER 8
Hidden in Plain Sight

When I was a kid, I met a missionary who visited the little Methodist Church in the town where we grew up. This missionary told us a story about his experiences in China during the Japanese invasion.

He said that when the Japanese invaded China they arrived at the mission home where the missionaries were living and forced all the people in the mission to come out of the house.

He described the Japanese soldiers with their bayonets. During that war, certain Japanese soldiers were notorious for bayoneting people, including women and children. This missionary said when everyone came out of the mission house; these Japanese soldiers were ready to bayonet the missionaries, as well as all the followers in the compound.

He described how the soldiers stood, with their guns poised, ready to begin bayoneting. He looked up to heaven and said, "*Oh God, nobody here's afraid to die, but God we entreat you, we ask you to intercede for us and help us*."

He said that he just prayed that small, simple prayer, but when he looked at the commander of the Japanese force, he saw the commander's eyes began to get big. The commander began to back up. He could see that the other soldiers were feeling funny, and they began backing up as well. He could see sheer terror on their faces.

Little by little, they just kept backing up. Some of them dropped their guns and began running as fast as they could, away, into the forest.

The missionary said that they stood there, all the missionaries and Chinese converts and they just watched the soldiers running away. Later some of the missionaries met a few of those Japanese soldiers who spoke to them of 'huge *men with huge swords that were standing behind them in that compound'*.

Your present life and eternal future is at stake!

Oh my God! Somewhere, sometime, we're going to have to get real about what Christianity is all about. We're going to have to see Jesus! We can't keep playing church. We can't keep playing with the things that are real. We can't. Because one day, we're going to *see* the Lord and we're going to *need* the Lord. We don't want to leave learning to see Jesus until it's too late!

The Bible says that there are going to be people to whom He's going to say, "*Depart from Me, I never knew you.*"

A lot of those people, if you read the scripture, were people who thought they *did* know Him. I know this kind of talk is not popular.. I know it's not and I don't enjoy it. I love to talk about all the exciting, positive stuff. I like to encourage people. That's my heart. That's what I feel is my calling. I really do. I want to encourage. I don't want to beat up anybody. Why would I? You've probably already beaten yourself up badly enough. Am I not telling the truth?

Your opportunity is now, don't let feeling bad keep you from Jesus! He loves you!

Nobody can beat you up worse than you beat up yourself. So that's the last thing I want to do, but I have to tell you about this. If we don't deal with this, the opportunity to see Jesus may pass you by and you'll miss it.

If you aren't serious about this, and you really don't want to deal with it, God will give you your wish. He will let you go your way and let you do what you want to do. He won't force you to take note of Him. But He's bringing you this opportunity to see that you need to see Jesus…get to know Him and hear what He's telling you.

Sometime, what you see with your eyes is only part of the story… it's not over till it's over!

I love the story of the two disciples that were on the road to Emmaus. This story is found in Luke 24 and it talks about the 3rd day after Jesus was crucified. Two of Jesus' disciples were walking on the road to Emmaus. They're walking along, bummed out and hurting. They're thinking about how they had followed Jesus all these years. Three amazing years that He was on earth. They'd had close contact with Him while He was on earth, and now they were tremendously hurt and disappointed, because they'd expected so much from Him.

But then contrary to what they'd expected, they had watched Him die a gruesome death on Calvary's cross. They'd watched Him being buried, just days before. Watched Him being put into that tomb, and then watched as the stone was rolled over the tomb's mouth. It looked as if it was all over. They felt that their hope was gone as they walked along that road.

You know, sometimes we give up too soon. Can you agree with that? Sometimes we give up too soon. Sometimes we give up on people too soon. Sometimes we give up on situations too soon.

We need to stay put and keep our faith staunch in Jesus, continuing to believe in Him, even when it seems that all hope is gone.

Doubt will keep you blind, even when Jesus is walking right next to you. On that road to Emmaus, the disciples were walking, talking back and forth with one another. But, what they were really doing, was voicing a lot of unbelief to one another, saying things like, "*Oh man, you know, I thought Jesus was going to rise up and set Israel free. And then, even at the end, I thought as we watched Him on the cross that surely, He was just going to get off. Now it seems that everything we've believed in these last few years is gone*!"

The Bible says that Jesus began to walk alongside them. As He's walked alongside them, He keeps them from seeing who He is. Now it says in Luke 24: "*their eyes were holden so that they should not know Him.*"

The word 'holden' here means that Jesus took control of what they could see. Now I want you to take note of this word 'holden'. Jesus could keep them from seeing certain things. They couldn't see who He was. They couldn't recognize Him.

Now this is really important: these men are walking with Jesus, having a conversation with Him, but they don't recognize Him. Now why didn't Jesus just walk up to them and say, "*Hey boys! Here I am. Look at the wounds in My hands. Look at the wounds in My feet. Look at the wound in My side. Look! Look! I'm here, I've risen.*"

Why didn't He do that? That's not how it happened. What did happen? Jesus begins walking with them. What He begins to do is to talk to them as if He's a stranger. He begins to go through the scriptures with them. He begins to go through the Word of God explaining the scriptures to them and says, "*Wasn't it right that Jesus went to the cross and died*?"

Believe what God says and you'll never be without hope.

He spoke to them from the Word of God. He explained the meaning of the scriptures to them so that they would understand what had happened to Jesus and believe. As He does this, something begins to happen inside the disciples. Suddenly, they move from the low, doubting, hopeless state of mind they were in and they begin to see the truth and get excited. They begin to feel better.

You know, the Word of God will do that to you. It'll make you feel better. They begin to find a little hope. Their hope began to grow as they walked and talked with this Man.

The Bible says that when they came to the place where they were going to stop for the night, Jesus acted as if he was going to continue further on the road. In effect He says, "*You boys take care and have a good night, enjoy your supper and I'll see you,*" and He prepares to leave them.

It then says that they 'constrained' Him. Now it's not hard to understand what that word means. It means they were holding onto Him to such a degree that it was almost if they were tying Him up, "*No, no, no! You've got to come with us. Come on! No, please don't go on, come with us tonight. It's too late to go on.*"

When they began to understand the scriptures, they became excited. It was as if they had new life imparted to them, and they didn't want to let this 'stranger' go. They wanted more of the truth and the encouragement He was giving them. That's the way it is when you begin to really see Jesus and adhere to His Word.

CHAPTER 9
Focus, Focus, Focus

When was the last time you had one of those 'I won't let You go' moments? Have you ever been so blessed and felt God so strongly that you say, "Oh God, please don't go… please don't go… Oh God, if I could stay in this moment just forever, God, I'd never leave this place?"

Recently, we had a little revival in our church. One Saturday night, we were praying for people to get filled with the Holy Ghost. I want to tell you, something happened that night. It was one of those 'I won't let You go' moments!

People just didn't want to go home. People were here crying and just walking around and enjoying His presence. No one was saying, "*You know what, that sermon sure was long.*" Something happened. The power of God was moving. People were at the front of the church. I was standing, watching what was happening, enjoying feeling God move. People were crying in tongues… worshipping…something broke loose in this place and people just wanted to stay around. You know why people stayed around? Because that stuff feels good…it feels good when you focus on Jesus. The Bible says, "*Draw near to Him and He will draw near to you.*" The disciples on the road to Emmaus were telling Jesus, "*You've got to come with us.*" They still didn't recognize Him, but the Word in Itself had encouraged them. But when they sat down to eat, and He broke the bread, their eyes were opened.

Now, what I want to tell you is this, if you want to be a fool, God will allow you to stay blind. I know you don't like that, but this is the Word of God. The Bible says, '*with their ears they won't hear, with their eyes they won't see*"

Do you remember those people that Jesus tells to depart from Him? Do you know who those people are? They're the people who're playing games. They don't want to hear and see.

They don't want to make the effort or spend the time necessary to focus on Jesus. If you don't want to hear and see, then the blindness and the deafness to the Lord will get worse than it already is.

But, these disciples, on the road to Emmaus, encouraged by the Word, wanted to see and they had 'their eyes opened.'

If you can't see Jesus, stop whatever you're doing and ask God to open your eyes.

They had their eyes opened. You know what that means? **Have you ever read, in the book of James, where it says that if you lack wisdom, if you need wisdom, ask God for wisdom and He'll give it to you?** This is in the first chapter of James.

This means He'll open your eyes and help you to understand what's happening and see what needs to be done in your life. These disciples were given wisdom. Their eyes were opened up and then they knew Him and then He disappeared from their physical sight.

They said to one another – note this –"*Did not our hearts burn within us while He talked with us along the way and while He opened to us the scriptures.*" Oh my! "*Didn't our hearts burn within us? Didn't our hearts burn within us?"*

You can't get around Jesus and not have your heart burn, unless something's wrong. What could be wrong? If you're in His presence, and you're heart's not burning within you, what could be wrong?

What's wrong is that you're busy cooking. You're busy looking for kudos for the gravy and the cranberry sauce! But that stuff, the busyness of life, is not important – you can't let it be that important to you if you want to have your eyes opened to see who He really is.

You'll 'hear' and 'see' things that other people don't when you're focused on Jesus

There's a certain brother and sister I have been talking with a lot lately. This brother said something to me recently that made me realize again how important it is to listen for and to see Jesus. One day, earlier in the week, God began dealing with me about this brother. I didn't know why, but God just began to put him on my heart.

The way I usually find out, in a situation like that, whether it's God or not that's talking to me, is by saying, "*Lord if this is you, and You want me to call brother so-and-so, I'll sure do that.*" and then, I just go on with my day. On this particular occasion, I did this and then I went on with my day, but the feeling just kept on and on… '*you need to speak this day to brother so-and-so'*.

Eventually, I decided to send him a text message. Now, I've watched all the young people text messaging each other. These are kids that struggle to learn anything at school, but they can work those phones faster than anything in the world. Have you ever seen them? Click, click, click. Just as fast as can be.

So, I'm texting this brother…and it took me a good half an hour just to get the little message done. But, finally, I sent it to him and he sends a text back to me saying, "*Pastor this came exactly at the right time!* " After this, we were talking one night, and he was sharing with me about his situation. He said, "You didn't know…but your message came just at the right time."

Am I just trying to show myself as being spiritual? No not at all. But I'm going to tell you, I don't play with this. I don't take it lightly. The spiritual is real. This Word of God is real to me. My life with God is real. I don't play games with this. This means something important to me.

God will make a way where there is no way… Why is it so real to me? I used to be in a place where I couldn't get out by myself and God got me out. I was in a place where *nobody* could help me, nobody had any way or any words to rescue me, but God got me out.

I watched God turn my family around when no one else could turn them around. God got me out of a hole that no one else could.

It's so real that I pray for my kids and I pray for my grandkids. I pray for my relatives. I pray for people I come in contact with. I even see people on the street sometimes and I pray for them. I pray. Why? Because I *know* that prayer makes a difference and I know that God will rescue people because we pray. I'm very serious about this.

It doesn't matter how seemingly hopeless your situation is, or how far down you feel, it's not hopeless for God. The Bible says in Matthew 19:26, "*With men this is impossible, but all things are possible with God.*"

It also says in Mark 9:23, "*all things are possible to him who believes...*"

All it requires for you to step out of the boat, walk on the water, right on top of those troubles, is to believe that God can, and will help you. That He is above every circumstance and bad situation in your life. That He loves you and will help you, if you will just believe that, the Bible says that He will.

The only thing that God requires of you is that you trust Him. In Hebrews 11:6 it says, "*But without faith it is impossible to please Him, for he that cometh to God must believe that He is and that He is a rewarder of them that diligently seek Him.*"

We have to 'diligently' seek Him. That means we must stick to it. We must look to Him all the time. Consistently. Not giving up when the going gets tough or it seems that the situation isn't changing. This scripture says that He will then reward us. How will He reward us? By giving us wisdom. By showing us what to do to get out of the hole we're in. By letting us see Him and getting to know Him better, through understanding His word and His ways more and more. He's not going to show Himself to someone who only calls out to Him every time they get into trouble and then as soon as they get out of trouble, they just ignore Him again.

He wants a close, loving relationship with us.
He's not there just for 'fire insurance'.

But even if that's been you in the past...or maybe you've never called out to Him for help before, or never expected Him to help you before, you can call to Him right now. Maybe your life is going fine. Maybe it's a disaster. Even if it's great now, He can make it greater. But, if it's a disaster, don't worry. No matter how the odds are stacked against you right now, God can change your situation in an instant. As a man once said, "God + me = a majority"[2].

The most important thing you should do, if you haven't already done it, is to ask Jesus to come and live in your heart and make a decision to trust Him to look after you from now on.

PART THREE
The Odds
Don't Matter

"The Lord is with you, mighty warrior," he said. I looked over my shoulder to see what great person he was talking to. There weren't any mighty warriors around that I knew. At least, not amongst the children of Israel right at that moment. There wasn't anyone there. Except me. I looked at him, He looked at me. Me? Me? I laughed. Bitterly. "But sir, if the Lord is with us, why has all this happened to us? Where are all His wonders that our fathers told us when they said, 'Did not the Lord bring us up out of Egypt?' But now... now the Lord has abandoned us and put us into the hand of the Midian." The Lord turned to me and said, "Go in the strength you have and save Israel out of Midian's hand. Am I not sending you?" I nearly choked. Me!? In MY strength? "But Lord, how can I *save Israel? My clan is the weakest in Manasseh, and I am the least in my family." What a joke! Doesn't he know I'm Gideon the most cowardly son of Joash? He answered, "*I *will be with you and you will strike down all the Midianites together."*

Oh...my...gosh. Me? Here I am, hiding in the winepress because of those marauding bandits, too scared to show myself in daylight and I'm *going to strike them down all together...? I must be hallucinating. I've got to test this.*

"So... if I've found favor in your

eyes, give me a sign it's really You talking to me. Please, don't go away until I come back and bring my offering and set it before you."

He nodded. "I'll wait."

I ran off to prepare a goat and bread. It'd take a while. Surely by the time I got back, he'd have grown tired of the joke and disappeared.

Anyone who thought I was a mighty warrior had to be a figment of my imagination... or have a warped sense of humor.

But no. When I got back he was still there. Not only that, but he took the offering, touched his staff to it and the whole lot went up in smoke. THEN he disappeared.

I'd never been so scared in my life. I fell on my face in terror crying, "Ah! Sovereign Lord! I have seen the Angel of the Lord face to face!" I knew that no man can see Him face to face and live. I was done for.

But He said, "Peace, do not be afraid. You are not going to die."

CHAPTER 10
The Battle Belongs to the Lord

There's a very interesting story about a man called Gideon, in Judges Chapter 6. I want to show you some things in this story that aren't perhaps the obvious things that you first think of when you initially read it.

It's a wonderful story, and a good read, but there are things in there that, if you see them, will help you understand how the impossible in your life can become possible.

I believe the things I'm about to share with you will minister to you in a big way. I'm going to focus on verse 34. Though I'll touch on other verses as I share with you, verse 34 holds the key to some strong encouragement. It says, "*But the Spirit of the Lord came upon Gideon and he blew a trumpet and Abiezer was gathered after him.*"

Now if you read the whole story, you'll find that other people, besides the clan of Abiezer also came to join him, but the thing I want you to notice in particular is, "*...the Spirit of the Lord came upon Gideon...*"

If you read this verse in the Amplified Version of the Bible, it puts it like this: '*the Spirit of the Lord clothed Gideon with Himself.*"

In other words, the Spirit of the Lord came and covered Gideon. When this took place, it just swept Gideon up and caused him to do things he wasn't capable of doing by himself in the natural.

I want to tell you something very exciting, and I want you to pay careful attention to this. This same kind of 'covering' by the Spirit of the Lord can happen *today* in our world. It can happen to you and to me. We read things in the Bible and we tend to say, "*Oh that was wonderful for back then.*" But what I want to tell you is it's *not* just for back then.

The Bible says, "*Jesus Christ the same, yesterday, today and forever.*" What does that mean? That means that God was full of power, back then, He's still full of power now and He's always going to be that way, forever.

But…you can't just flip a switch to turn the Power on.

The problem with us, today, is that we're so impatient about everything. We don't want to take the time to really dig into things. When we go to work and do whatever it is that we do at work, we know that it takes a certain amount of time to complete certain tasks. We all know that. It doesn't matter if we're washing cars or building jet planes, it takes time to put things together.

The thing is, we've got to have a hunger inside our spirit that drives us to spend the time necessary to receive from God. We have to get to the point where we become tenacious. Where we don't allow things that are happening around us to dominate us or distract us. Where we're prepared to wait on God for help. Now, when we get like that, God comes and covers and overshadows us and He causes us to mount up to levels we've never, ever been before.

So what am I saying? I'm saying that God can break any yoke, God can break any habit, God can break any situation, if we will stay on our knees and stay in faith before Him, saying, "God, I'm not moving until I hear from you!" But most of us are impatient and we want things right away.

The main reason we get into trouble in the first place, is that we do the wrong things.

Now, in this story about Gideon, it's interesting to me, that in the very first verse of Chapter 6 it says, "*the children of Israel did evil in the eyes of the Lord.*"

Whenever we go against what God is doing, we put ourselves in a place of much hurt, of much pain, of much misdirection, of much sorrow; and we bring on ourselves a lot of things we're going to have to work through later on in life.

In Gideon's story, the Israelites had, over time, got to a place where they thought that they were so good and had everything together so well, that they forgot God. How many of us forget God when we're in the good times? Most of us, when we're experiencing good times and things are going great, forget God.

Forgetting the Lord will bring constant trouble.

Recently, one of my team said, "God don't make me so rich that I forget you, but not so poor that I have to beg and steal." They were paraphrasing Proverbs 30:8,9.

We were talking about how many of us, when things are going well and God has blessed us to the hilt; tend to quickly forget who blessed us and how we got where we are. That's what happened with the children of Israel. They forgot about the Lord and they did evil in His sight.

As I was studying this, I read further through Judges Chapters 6, 7 and 8, I began to see what the evil was that they did, was and I believe it's going to really surprise you, when you see this.

It wasn't so much that the children of Israel were doing horrendous things. The evil that they did in the sight of the Lord was that they *forgot who blessed them.* They began to turn a blind eye to God. They began to think, "*Wow, everything is wonderful, life is great and we really don't have to worry about God.*

But, you always have to keep your mind on God. The Bible says that as they began to move away from under the covering, or protection of the Lord, this allowed the Midianites to come and torment them.

It's significant that the very word 'Midian' or "Midianites' means strife or contention. It means that as the children of Israel walked away from God and began to do their own thing, their actions allowed a group of people, the nation of Midianites, to come in against them, bringing them nothing but strife and contention.

Strife and contention will rob us of blessing.

How many of us know what strife is firsthand? How many of us have known contention in our lives? How many of us have experienced the frustration strife and contention bring?

When strife and contention are present, things just don't seem to work right. Have you noticed? When there's strife and contention, everything you put your hand to just seems to fall apart. Or you pick up this and lose that. Nothing seems to work in your life.

The Bible says that when the children of Israel would raise their crops, the Midianites would come in and take them all. Not only the Midianites, but the Amalekites and the children of the East. These foreign nations took everything from them. So no matter how hard they worked, or what they gathered, something would come in and take it from them.

I remember years ago when I was working for Hewlett-Packard. At that time, we only had our two older boys, who were both little. Twice a year, Hewlett-Packard gave us a profit sharing check. I used to love those profit sharing checks and really looked forward to them. Hewlett-Packard would give us one in summer and one at Christmas time.

At this time, I had just got my profit sharing check when Debbie told me that we had to go to wash some clothes at the Laundromat. We didn't even have a washer and dryer then. So, off we went to the Laundromat.

As Debbie and I were getting clothes out of the car and carrying them into the Laundromat, I remember saying to the boys, "*Boys, just sit there, we'll get you right out.*" We weren't more than a few feet away from the car. I don't remember which one of them did it, but one of them got up behind the wheel of my car, an old Buick, pulled it out of gear and that bad boy rolled down the parking lot and right into this custom made Cadillac. An immaculate Cadillac.

I think if I hadn't been bigger than the guy in the Cadillac, he'd have whipped me good! He was so cross! He just wanted to cry. It was a beautiful car. My old Buick rolled right into it… BAM!

So that's how we spent our little profit sharing check - it went to fix that man's car. We didn't get to use that money at all. And I can remember going over and over it in my mind, thinking things like, "*My God, seems like whenever I can get my hands on something, something comes and takes it away*!"

Remembering God's provision with gratitude will keep us covered by His protection.

I'm going to tell you something: if you're experiencing that kind of thing, check yourself! Check your relationship with God. I'm not saying this is always the case when something like this happens, but it's worth checking yourself.

When we get to the place where we think we're doing it all on our own and we don't have to look to God anymore, or trust God the way we did in times past, it opens the door to a lot of things allowing them to come in your life and cause you strife and contention. The reason is that you're forgetting the Lord.

Wouldn't you get mad at your children if they became millionaires and forgot that you were the one that raised them? If they forgot that for years, you were the one who got up and changed their dirty diapers in the middle of the night? But now that they're rich, they don't know you anymore. They don't appreciate anything you've done for them in the past and they think they don't need you now.

Don't forget that God is the One who causes you to succeed.

It always amazes me how ungrateful people are and how they like to run down the person who causes them to succeed. I was watching the news the other day and there was a story on about Michael Jackson.

Somehow, they always make the Jackson's father look like a dog. They focus on how hard this father was on the Jackson kids. Maybe he was, I don't know. But the thing I've always seen is that if Joe Jackson hadn't been hard on those kids, they would never have become famous the way they did.

People like to complain about how bad the person was who caused them to succeed and ignore what that person did to help them succeed. Well,

God is the one who causes you to succeed and you'd better not forget it. Because, when you forget Him, you walk out from under His protection and you face the things that God has been taking care of every day for you.

The Bible says that one of the tribes that came against Gideon and his people were the Amalekites. The word 'Amalekite' means 'dweller of the valley.' Literally, it means that these people lived in depression and despair. It was as if they were continually passing through a dread. The Amalekites lived in that valley of depression and despair, yet they would come up out of that valley to plunder the Israelites riches and their goods.

Don't focus on the bad, hurtful things in life unless you want to stay in that bad, hurtful place.

When I read that about the children of Israel, I begin to think how many of us allow our attitudes and depressions to take us through all kinds of rivers and valleys and bad places where we don't want to go. We become so focused on the things that get us down that we quit looking at God.

When we focus on the bad things, this focus will draw us into areas that hurt us and destroy our lives. If we look at the bad things in our lives with such intense focus and attention, over a period of time, they will overcome us. Quit looking at those things and look to God.

I remember years ago when the movie 'Schindler's List' came out, I went to see it by myself. Going into the movie theatre I noticed that theatre was filled with mostly older people. There were not many people my age. (When I told this story at church I saw some of the kids looking at me, thinking "*Your age... my God! They must've really been old in that place*.")

As I watched Schindler's List, I began to hear people whimpering all around me. During certain scenes in the movie, I saw some of these older people cover their eyes and drop their heads. I could hear some people crying and I could hear some saying, "*I remember that*."

As those people were watching the movie, it was taking them back to a place that held hurt for them. It was taking them back to a place where they had been hurt and they were feeling that same hurt, over and over again, as they watched that movie.

That's the way you and I are. We get the spirit of the Amalekites on us and we keep going back, mentally viewing something that reminds us of hurt. We've got to come out of that! The Bible says that the children of Israel did evil in the sight of the Lord, and the first evil they did, was that they kept looking at the past.

Some of us can't stop living in the past. Get out of the past! We keep saying, "*I do that because of this...I can never marry again because of that person...I can never trust this type of person again because someone like that hurt me. I can never go on because...*" and we keep living in the past where our destruction is, where our hurt is. The problem is that if we stay there, if we keep living in the past, we're never going to see the power of God.

I want to tell you that our hearts are not beating today, we're not alive today, to dwell in a place where we've already been a million times. We're alive to step into something new. To walk into something good. Something that's on fire. Something that's real.

When we take our focus off God we become impoverished.

In Judges Chapter 6, it says that Israel was greatly impoverished because of the Midianites. As a result, the children of Israel cried unto the Lord. If you look at the word 'impoverished', it means that they were less, they were no longer equal to everybody around them.

The Bible gives the idea that when you walk away from God, you're no longer equal to everybody else.

What does that mean? It means that whenever you take a step away from the Lord, you're taking a step down. Whenever you take a step away from the Lord, you're taking a step lower. You're accepting the worst instead of the best God has for you. Jesus didn't die on Calvary's cross to have you stay a sinner. Jesus didn't die on Calvary's cross to have you stay bound by something or someone. Jesus died on Calvary to set you free. To set you FREE. Not so that you're bound by something that He has already defeated.

But, instead of experiencing the freedom He has given us, today many of us have come to the place where we're impoverished. When we cry out to the Lord, the one thing God will do is He will always send a prophet to talk to us before our change, our deliverance, comes.

CHAPTER 11
God Will Always Send a Prophet

When you call out to God for help, He will always send a prophet who's anointed by the Holy Spirit and this prophet will speak God's words to you before your deliverance comes.

You are reading these words right now by divine appointment. God has connected you with this book, with this old Pastor, because this is your appointment, a divine appointment with God. (I hope you don't get mad at me and think I have a big head.) I tell you this: God has appointed me to tell you to come out of your bondage. He sent you this book to tell you to come out of that hole you're in.

When God appointed Gideon to deliver the Israelites, they had become impoverished. The children of Israel were afraid of the heathens around them. The Midianites, the Amalekites and the children of the East continually plundered everything they had.

Every time they were about to harvest their crops, they would be raided. The children of Israel began to dig caves and holes in the mountains for strongholds to try to hide away and get some relief from their enemies.

When we walk away from God, we'll always find ourselves hiding from predators, both spiritual and in the flesh. We'll find it hard to keep our faith intact. Things will get worse and worse and worse until we cry out to the Lord. Then, when we do, God will send someone to tell us that He will bring us out. *I'm* telling you this today: *God wants to bring you out*!

God loves you so much that He wants you to get out of where you are. The children of Israel did horrible things. They walked away from God even after He had done miracles for them. They scoffed and laughed at what He had done and yet, God still heard them when they cried out to Him for help, and He sent them a prophet. The prophet came and spoke to these people under the influence of the Holy Spirit.

Sometimes, I turn on the Christian Television, and I watch some of these people on TV. I watch how they minister. Some of them are spooky, the way they move. They look at people and say, "*I see this...* " and they begin to speak about what they are 'seeing'.

Now I'm not saying this to make fun of them, believe me. But, even though sometimes when you watch these things, you may wonder if they're for real, I do know this: there are times when I know and feel, the Spirit of God stronger than I do at other times. There are times when I know things that I don't always know in the normal, natural course of events. I'm not trying to lift myself up, I'm just being honest. It does not happen all the time, nor, to be honest, does it happen that often. But sometimes, God will speak to my heart and say, "*Tell this person this. Tell them that. Tell them they need to go this way, or do this*."

There are times when God speaks to me about someone because He loves the other person so much. At times, He'll come and deal with my heart so strongly that I can't get away until I speak those words of encouragement to that person so that they can get out of the hole they're in. That's how powerful God can be.

If God spoke through donkeys, surely He can speak through me. Sometimes God will show me things that I could never have known in the natural. At times, God has sent me to places where I wouldn't normally be going, just so that I could be there at a particular time and do a specific thing for Him. Why? Because He loves people enough to get them out of the trouble.

Remember the good things God has already done for you….

When you call out to the Lord for help, He sends a prophet. The next thing He'll do is to remind us of how things were in contrast to how they are now. God will always remind us of when we were blessed. Can you remember when you were blessed? Perhaps you are blessed now.

Whenever we remember the past, we reminisce, "*Oh I remember when I had hair... I remember back when I looked like this.*" We even keep a favorite picture of us from the past when we really looked good, the kind of picture where we had our stuff together. We just had that *look*. We keep history like this around because it takes us back to a place where we were on top of things.

I've got a few pictures of me like that. There's one of me standing with a bass guitar. My hair was really, really long. I had my nightclub suit on and I'm just *standing* there, looking good. That's one of my favorite pictures. It's been torn and cracked and I just keep repairing it, because it's one of my favorite pictures.

We like to reminisce about the good times. One Friday night, the Church music team had finished practicing but we stayed another hour talking about the 'old days'. We were throwing stories back and forth… "*Yeah and I remember…*"

When I went home that night, I said "*Oh God, I'm so thankful for how things were, but Lord, I want that kind of anointing and power on me now. I don't want to live in the past talking about what went on then. I want it now and I want to see You moving in my life, now, fresh, new and powerful.*"

I told God when I came back into the ministry that I didn't want to come back unless I could see His power working in people's lives. I wanted to see change. I still want to see change.

As far as God is concerned, fear is disobedience…
it's thinking something or someone else is more powerful than He is.

Now, in Judges 6:10, God explains the problem to the children of Israel. He says, *"Now I say unto you I am the Lord your God. Fear not the gods of the Amorites in whose land you dwell. But you have not obeyed My voice."*

The problem, the Bible tells us, was that the people of the east were pushed out of the land so that the Israelites could have their land when they came out of Egypt.

The word 'Amorite' means 'speaking something in your mind or your heart'.

He reminds the children of Israel, "*I gave you the land of the Amorites, but* ***I told you to fear not the gods of the Amorites****.*"

Now I want you to look at this verse closely, *"I say unto you, I am the Lord your God. Fear not the gods of the Amorites in whose land you dwell* ***but you have not obeyed my voice."***

Sometimes you take less than you're supposed to and by doing so, you make the 'less' you've taken become a curse in your life. God told the children of Israel, "*When I gave you this land, I told you not to be afraid of their gods*." But, they were afraid of the Amorite gods anyway. Why were they afraid of the Amorite gods?

Because, the children of Israel were looking with natural eyes. They saw what the Amorites were doing to them and they began to believe that the Amorite's gods were stronger than their own God who had brought them out of Egypt. Instead of remembering all the miracles God had done for them, they focused on what the Amorites and Midianites were doing to them now.

They became so afraid of these heathens that they began to think their gods were more powerful than the Israelites own God. They became impoverished in themselves… they began to think they were not equal to the heathens around them.

How many times do you look at people that are making it and are successful today and see that they're not Christians? They don't love the Lord, but they're doing great, and you look at them and ask, "*Well I'm a Christian, God, how come I'm not doing that? God, I'm supposed to have your favor, I'm supposed to have these miracles. God, what's going on*?"

What you're doing, is you're looking at their gods, and you're putting your God down. If you want to be successful, if you want to go over the top, then you stay with *our* God and He will carry you all the way through.

This is what He's talking about. He said, "*You have not obeyed my voice. You're looking at their gods and you've become afraid of them. Not only have you become afraid of their gods, you've adopted their gods.*"

You have adopted their gods. You have adopted their ways. You have adopted the things they do. Now you're doing the very same things as the non-Christian and that makes you no different from them.

CHAPTER 12
The Lord Will Send a Deliverer

We're people of faith. We're people who do the supernatural. We're people who do things that normal people cannot do because of the God we serve. That's why, when we are walking through life, being a Christian, we need to walk in joy.

The joy of the Lord is our strength.

We need to walk in joy. Because why would someone want to give their heart to God and be miserable, like most Christians seem to be?

Recently a group of us at church, were talking about an old man who would stand out in the street and preach. He was dressed in disheveled clothes, looking horrible, preaching about God and telling everybody they were going to hell. When people look at somebody like that, they say, "*I sure don't want what he's got. My God, whatever he's got I don't want. I don't need that.*"

That's why God wants us to walk in joy, victory and balance because it is these things that draw the lost to us to see what our God is all about.

I've read several times about how they used to kill Christians in Roman arenas. Even as they were being brutally killed, these Christians held fast to their trust in God and died well. These people were walking in faith and in power. When carnivorous animals' or men would kill them, they died with dignity. History says that for every Christian they killed, a thousand sinners in the arena audience would get saved.

Where's our honor, where's our dignity? We are serving the living God. We are not to be beggars, or people running around and acting like we don't have a way, because we do have a way. We should not be like someone who's serving a god who's weak. The trouble is that we've been just like the children of Israel to whom He said, "*but you have not obeyed my voice*."

The Lord will send a deliverer who understands what we're facing.

When the children of Israel called out to God, God sent a prophet and a deliverer. Gideon was the deliverer. In Judges 6:14, it says, "*And the Lord looked upon him and said, "Go in* ***thy might*** *and* ***thou*** *shalt save Israel from the hands of the Midianites, have I not sent thee?"*

A deliverer comes from the same trouble we've been in. He knows what we're facing. The interesting thing about that verse is He says to Gideon, "*Go in* ***your*** *might.*" What does He mean by this, "*Go in your might*?"

God won't move if we won't.

When God tells us to do something, most of us say, "*God, I want to accomplish this, but oh God, just open the door for me*." We pray those prayers, don't we? "*God, I know this is in my heart. God, I know you've called me, but now God I'm just going to wait on you. Until you do something God, I'm here, waiting on you.*"

That's not what He told Gideon. He told Gideon "*I want* ***you*** *to deliver the children of Israel.*" Gideon didn't say, "*Okay...well, God, when you get ready to do that I'm behind the wine press here, trampling out the grapes; hiding. Winnowing out a little bit of wheat trying to feed my family.*"

That's not what happened. He said, "*Gideon, go in* ***your*** *might.*" What does that mean? It means that when God has given you a mandate, when God has given you a call, when God has sent you to do something, that means ***you*** *get up off your bottom and* ***you*** *get busy*. It means that you begin to walk differently. It means that you walk in amongst the impossible and you make it possible. *It means that you fear no one.*

Come boldly to the throne of grace.

That means that you walk into the situation and you begin to speak things. People may say to you, "*My gosh, why are you doing that*?" I know that's embarrassing. But so what? You'll get over being embarrassed.

My wife and I were talking about this the other night, driving in the car. We were talking about our kids. One of our boys always tells us, "*Wow, Mom and Dad, you guys talk to everybody.*" And we do. If we don't know something, we ask questions. I mean, we'll walk right up and say to somebody, "*How do you do that?*"

When we do that, our kids are embarrassed, saying, "*Mom! Stop it! Mom! Don't do that!*" My wife just responds, "*If I don't know, I'm going to ask.*" She says, "*I don't care if they think I'm crazy. They're not going to see me again so why should I care?*"

Some of us have been denied because we're too embarrassed to ask, or to do what God has told us to do. God says, "*Come boldly to the throne of grace.*" Some of us are being denied because we're too embarrassed, too withdrawn, and too timid. Now, I'm quite a withdrawn person. I really am. But, when I need something, I'm going to get it and I'll go wherever I have to go, to get it.

And that's what God meant when He said, "*go in your might.*" He said, "*Gideon get up and begin to act differently because I'm with you. Get up and do things like you've never done before. Get in. Experience things you've never experienced before*".

CHAPTER 13
Don't Be Part of the Problem

You know what my Dad used to do? My Dad used to walk the back roads of Kansas. He would walk because he was poor. His family was poor.

In the early days, when his father and his uncles went to homestead their place in Kansas, they got off the train and dug holes in the ground and that's where they lived until they were able to build houses. I've got the story and every time I get discouraged, I pull out that story and I read it.

When they got off that train, my Grandfather and his brothers had no place to live. They burrowed into the sides of little hills making dugouts where they would sleep and keep their belongings.

They covered the hole with some kind of blanket or tarpaulin. In the morning they'd wake up with rattlesnakes right there next to them. As soon as they'd wake up they'd sling those snakes outside. They lived like that until they built a house. That land in Kansas, that they homesteaded, is still in the Moon name today.

When I think of this story, it makes me realize that this is where we often miss it. We miss it, because we don't ever want to get on the train and go dig a hole and start something. We're too afraid.

Get up and act like a child of the

Father.

This was one of the evils of the children of Israel. They were acting as if they did not know God. Some of us act like we don't know God. Some of us act like we don't know our parents.

But, come on, we've got to do something. Do you hear me? What we've got to do is rise up and become tired of being denied. We've got to rise up and say what needs to be said and do what needs to be done.

Recently, a brother was telling me about the first job he got in trucking. He said he kept asking the company boss for a job. He kept asking, until this man called him up and gave him the job. When this man called, he said, "*I'm tired of you calling me.*" This brother got the job. Now, if you were that brother, what would you care that the boss got tired and mad? You got the job!

Mostly, we don't want to go in our might. We're too lazy, or too afraid of doing the wrong thing, or of upsetting somebody. We want the answer to our problem to just drop into our lap. But this is what God told Gideon, and is now telling us to do, "*You've got to get up and stop being the victim.*"

Don't be a victim! Learn to fight for your God given blessings.

I spent a few days visiting with my mother recently and we had a good time. While I was there, I drove my Mom up to my sister and brother-in-law's church. As we were going back home, I drove by a Junior High School that I attended when I was a kid. This Junior High School is where I learned how to fight.

When I first started going to this school, I was not only an outsider, I was probably only the second or third black kid in the entire school. I had to walk two miles from home to get to school. And the whole two miles, I can remember dreading my arrival. Every day I'd arrive at school, and go inside and kids would jump on me.

I'd come home and I would tell my mother. Now, my mother was always good for a sob story, "*Mom, Mom, they hit me! Then they beat me up, Mom. Tore my coat, Mom.*"

Then, my mother would give me sympathy. You know how mothers are.

Until one day, my father got wind of it, and that was the end of that. He said, "*What!? Boy, don't you come home like that again.*"

I remember walking to school the next day. And sure enough, just like it had happened all the other times, I was jumped on as soon as I walked in. But this time, I started swinging. Whooph! Whooph! Whooph! Closed my eyes and swung as hard as I could. Whooph! Whooph! That's the way I used to fight. At the same time, I yelled, "Quit it.... *Stoooop*!"

Suddenly, as I was swinging, I got a little spring in my step. Bam! Bam! Suddenly I started dropping dudes and I realized, "*Man! I can fight! I can fight*!" From then on, when I'd go to school if anybody looked at me as if they were thinking about taking me on, I'd say, "*What are you looking at?*" and they'd back off. I made a niche for myself in that school and no one bothered me anymore!

Later when my siblings came to that school, nobody bothered them either. I didn't want to fight, but I had to or else I'd have continued being beaten up, or wedgied to death, and my lunch money taken everyday. But, I got to the point where I said, "*No, I'm not going to live like this anymore. I'm not going to let everybody just push me around.*"

I had to 'go in my might' and as I did, God began to help me. I didn't know I had the capabilities that I had. I was a big kid, but I didn't know that I could fight. But that day, I learned I could take a punch. Kids had been hitting me in the head all along and I was taking it. But then I realized that I could hit them back and I could hit them as hard as they hit me, or harder. Rolling in the snow, fighting with one kid, got my ear frost bitten, but I whipped that kid good! Matter of fact, that kid ended up becoming one of my best friends through life.

"*Go in thy might*", He's saying. Stop acting like a victim and a wimp. We've got to get up from where we are and do something.

Don't settle for less than Gods best.

After God told Gideon to go in his might, He went on to give him a specific task, "*Go and throw down the altars of Baal.*" One of the evils that was going on in Gideon's time was that the children of Israel were accepting less, and being cursed because they were accepting less.

Now it's important to see that *God got upset with these people because they were worshipping something a man had made*.

The heathen god Baal was carved out of wood. The Amalekites and Midianites and the children of the east came and bowed to this wooden god. Besides this wooden god, they had a tree, or pole, that was supposed to be this idol's wife, Asteroth. I believe they called her Astarte. They also used to grow groves of trees and they would worship these trees.

Then the children of Israel also began to worship these gods that they had chipped out of a rock, or carved out of a tree. They would actually bow down to them. God looked at this and He became angry. He was angry because His people were taking less instead of more. They were worshipping an idol and instead of the real thing.

You know what that's like? It's like instead of having a wife, settling for a blow-up doll. Now I can imagine you looking at me, thinking, "*Oh my God, Pastor, where ...*" No, I'm not trying to shock you, I'm just telling you the way it is. It's pretending you have something real when you don't.

Have you seen those people who drive in the traffic lanes where you're supposed to have at least two people in the car, but they don't? Some of these people have been caught. They try to pretend there are two people in the car by buying a dummy of a man with a little hat on and putting it next to them in the front seat.

Of course, they end up getting caught and fined because they're not supposed to be driving in those lanes. That's pretending. We don't have to pretend. We have the real thing. We have the real God, we don't need an idol.

There is no substitute for God.

You can have a lot of money, but you can also lose a lot of money quickly and then be broke and have nothing. You can have a lot of friends. But friends are fickle and sometimes, you can look around for the friends you had, and realize you don't have them anymore. So where are you? If you've relied on money and friends, you're alone. But if you've got God, He said, "*I'll never leave you or forsake you.*"

These were the evils that these people were doing. They did not obey God's voice. They feared the heathen gods. They began to worship these false gods. They went to these false gods for the help they needed, instead of to the one and only real God.

We have to be careful not to do evil the same way the children of Israel did evil. We have to make sure when we have a problem we go to the One who is real, who can help us.

That's why we shouldn't complain about our problems to everyone else. They can't help us. We have to take these things to God because He's the only one who can help us to change things from what they are now to the kind of abundant life He's promised us.

Imagine how upset we would be if we found our kids were telling their troubles to their friends at school, instead of to us as their parents. What if they believed that their friends had greater power to help them and cared more about them than their own parents did?

That's how God feels about us when we won't go to Him and ask Him for help and then trust Him to come through for us.

CHAPTER 14
The Kind of People God Won't Send to Help You!

There are certain people that God will *not* send to help you when you call to Him for help.

God won't send a crowd.

God won't help you with a whole crowd of people. We all like crowds, to a degree, don't we? I don't like crowds when they're just a crowd. But we always like a lot of friends around us when we want to feel better. You know what I'm saying?

Well, God's not going to have a whole crowd of people just come in and help you. Why? Because you'll think, "*My God, I've got so many friends, I'm such a wonderful person. Look at me. Everybody loves me. Surely they're going to help me.*"

No, God wants you to know that your help cometh from the Lord, not from people. He's not going to send a whole crowd of people to help you.

God won't send someone who's afraid.

He's also not going to send you people who are afraid. Matter of fact I'm really careful not to hang around with people who're always afraid.

Where do I get this from? After God called Gideon and finally motivated him to gather the different tribes around him to help him to go and whip the heathen armies, God did something interesting. God said to him, "*You've got too many people. Go down and get rid of some of those men, so that when you defeat the enemy, everyone will know that it's by My power, not yours.*"

The first men God told Gideon to get rid of were those that were afraid. He was told to ask them, "*How many of you are afraid? How many are afraid to go to battle*?" Twenty two thousand raised their hands and Gideon sent them all home.

Then God said, "*You still have too many with you. Take them down to the river and I'll separate them for you.*" So Gideon took them down to the river and God said, "*Tell them to drink.*"

Well some of them got down on all fours and stuck their heads in the water and drank with their mouths in the water. Now, most of us would probably have drunk it like that, down on all fours, our mouths in the water. It would've been easier.

But God said of the ones that did that, "*Send those ones home.*" All that were left were the three hundred men who pulled the water up in their hands to drink. God told Gideon, "*That's your army right there.*"

The people God sends are alert and on the ready.

Why did God choose only these men? Because, when you've got your head in the water or in the sand, you don't see anything. While your head's buried, things will come and attack you and destroy you.

But when you've got your eyes open and you're looking, you've got everything under control; you're alert, on the ready. That's how God's army has to be. So He sends those three hundred men. He sends only those people that aren't afraid. And He sends those people that are not bowing their knees to every problem that comes along.

As Christians, we have to be tough. Oh we're full of love… but we're tough! Full of love and we'll help and be a friend, but we're tough! You have to be tough to get through the many challenges of life. You have to be tough to hold the banner of God and say, "*I will not back up!*" We don't back up! We go forward. We only go forward!

Once the army was chosen, God told Gideon, '*Take a trumpet, take a pot, and take your shout.*" Note that God tells him to "*Take your trumpet.*" Then, God said, "*When I give you the signal, blow the trumpet.*"

The huge armies of the Midianites, the Amalekites and the children of the east were all spread out in the valley. Gideon gave the command, "*Blow your trumpets!*" Baaaahp! Baaaahp! They began to blow those trumpets.

It's a scary thing to hear trumpets blown like that. If you want to know how scary that is, talk to a veteran of the Korean War. During the Korean War, the Chinese would stand on the mountains and the hills before they attacked and they'd blow horns. At the sound of those horns, the Americans would freeze up in their foxholes. The sound of those horns was terrifying. It would reverberate through the air. Not just one horn, but many…a chilling fanfare! First they'd hear the horns, and then next thing they'd know, a horde of Chinese would come over the mountain and scare the Americans to death.

God told Gideon, "*Get your horn.*"

Now what he means for Gideon to do is to shake things up. The sound of the horns reverberating through the air shakes things up. God was saying to Gideon, "*Shake things up. Don't leave things the way they are. Shake them up. Come on.*"

The people God sends shine their lights as they go.

Then He says, "*Take your pot with you.*" Those jars they had were not small jars. They were big jars, big pots. Large pots. The army carried the pots . They put big torches inside those pots. Then, Gideon told his men, "*After you blow your trumpets, break those jars and pull out that light.*"

The Bible says in Matthew 5:16, *"Let your light so shine before men that they may see your good works and glorify your Father which is in heaven."*

It says, *"Neither do men light a candle and put it under a bushel but put it on a candlestick and it giveth light to all that are in the house."*

You see, we're supposed to shine the light of God on people, saying, "*We're coming in the Name of the Lord.*" God told Gideon that when they blew the trumpets, broke the jars and showed the lights, they were to shout, "For the Lord and for Gideon!" Now He didn't just say, "The Lord." He said “The Lord *and* Gideon.”

When Gideon and his men came down into the valley, the Bible says the men down in the valley got so scared that they began stabbing each other, killing each other with their swords.

The people God sends shout the victory!

Think about it. That would be like the Vice-President taking a shotgun and shooting his colleague in the face. That’s what happens when fear takes control.

God’s saying to us that we need to move in on the enemy like that. We have to move in on the enemy ‘for the Lord and for us’! We have to stop being ‘wimpified’. I know that’s not even a word, but it describes what I mean. We’ve got something to stand up with. We’ve got God. We have to shake things up and say, “*I serve the living God. And I will not, I will not be denied!*”

Odds don’t mean a thing. Odds don’t mean a thing when you’ve got God. When you’re clothed with the Spirit of God. Odds don’t mean a thing. What about you? What are you up against? Come out against that thing. Pull down the idol of fear! Be encouraged!

When you realize just how afraid the enemy is of you with God inside you, you can’t help but be encouraged. That’s why you have to stop talking yourself into being afraid.

“*Oh I could never accomplish that.*”

Stop saying that. You can accomplish whatever God said you can accomplish.

“*I’ll never be able to love again.*”

Stop saying that. Hallelujah. You have the God Who is Love living in you!

“*I’ll never be able to trust a man again.*”

Quit looking in the garbage and find a good man!

“*I’ll never sing again.*”

NO! You start singing and when they tell you to shut up, you keep singing. Keep singing until all of a sudden they can't help it and they say, "*Would you keep on singing? Would you keep on singing?*"

A little while ago, I was preaching at an old folk's home. Some of these old people were schizophrenic and had many other different things wrong with them. I was preaching and singing and this one old woman in the back kept saying, "*Want to sing again? Come on, are you going to sing again? Excuse me, excuse me, are you going to sing again?*"

I said, "*Honey, I'll sing when I come back.*"

"*Okay... we want to hear you sing again.*"

Oh you keep singing until people *want* to hear you sing. Don't you ever stop. Don't you ever quit. You have the right and the authority to sing and shout your victory!

Stop looking at the situation with your 'natural' eyes and start looking at it supernaturally. You worship the real God. The One who created everything. God doesn't expect you to do it in your own strength. He expects you to move out against the enemy with what you have now and He will step in and add His strength to yours! Remember: *"If God is for us, who can be against us"* (Romans 8:31).

God has given us the land, let's take it!

PART FOUR
The Proof of Real Christianity

*"**His divine power has given us everything that's necessary and suited to living a good and Godly life**. We access all this by getting to intimately know Him Who called us by and to His own glory and excellence (virtue).*

*Through His glory and power, **He's given us valuable and extremely powerful promises**. Believing and claiming these promises will help us share in His God nature, so that we can avoid being impacted by all the bad stuff that's happening in the world because of bad morals, greed and selfishness.*

To do this we have to tirelessly and consistently add our own efforts to these divine promises by taking every opportunity to practice using our faith in them. By continually believing in these promises and claiming them as our own and behaving in line with them, we'll develop virtue or power. As we start exercising this virtue we'll start to develop knowledge – in depth knowledge of how God really is... and how truly effective His promises are!

*As we begin to use this knowledge, we'll find we're **developing self-control.** Now, we think before we act and when we do act, we make the effort to act in a way that lines up with what we believe. Doing this consistently results in us becoming able to stay on track and stick to our values* *and beliefs, even when things don't go right as quickly as we'd like. We just stick with believing in those promises until nothing can move us away from them.*

The self-discipline of this kind of behavior helps us be more understanding and loving towards others, treating them gently and kindly, the way God treats us, instead of lashing out when they make us angry, as we used to do.

The end result is that we're steady, peaceful in God, kind and loving to everyone in all circumstances... in fact; to others we begin to look a lot like God. This is what it means to have 'Christian love'. We're supposed to show the world what He is really like!

As we live like this, cultivating these qualities, we'll find that we're becoming really useful to God and are able to achieve what He has planned for us. But most importantly, we'll have the most satisfying, exciting and uplifting relationship with our Lord Jesus Christ. We'll get to know Him fully – in all His goodness.

Anyone who doesn't do this is fooling themselves. They don't know God very well. Actually, they're blind to how wonderful He is and how great living with Him can be. This kind of person lives as if they're clueless about what Jesus actually did for them by cleansing them of their sins. They live as if they're still trapped in the consequences of that bad, old life, and they make no effort to take hold of the good life God has for them.

*This is why we must be really serious, in fact, eager, to take hold of what God has promised us. This cements the calling He's given us to be His children and live out the good plan He has for us. If we do this, we'll never stumble or fall. By taking hold of the divine promises He's provided, we're not just 'squeaking' into heaven...we're entering our Lord Jesus' eternal kingdom right now taking advantage of the rich, abundant way that He's provided for us" (***2 Peter 1:3-11 paraphrase mine).**

CHAPTER 15
Virtue? Goodness? What Does This Mean Today?

In the previous chapters, we've seen how much God has done for us and how He longs for us to simply come to Him in trust and in reliance on His goodness. However, as we've also seen, it's not only up to God. God does require us to take action in order to take advantage of the help He offers us. We've seen that He wants us to live a good life. A life free of worry and fear and failure.

Now, we're going to look at what we should be doing so that He can fully bless us. Come with me to 2 Peter 1. I want us to look at verses 1 – 8.

The Bible says, *"...According to His divine power hath given unto* ***us all things that pertain unto to life and Godliness*** *through the knowledge of Him that hath called us to glory and virtue whereby are given unto us exceeding great and precious promises"* (2 Peter 1:1-3).

In other words, God has given us all His great promises for us to use as we deal with Him.

"That by these you might be ***partakers*** *of the divine nature*" (2 Peter 1:4).

This is to help us become more like God, *"having escaped the corruption that is in the world through lust*" (2 Peter 1:4).

Now lust doesn't have to be anything nasty, it really just means 'desire'.

"And besides this, giving all diligence ***add*** *to your faith,* ***virtue*** *and to virtue, knowledge, and to knowledge, temperance, and to temperance, patience and to patience, Godliness and to Godliness, brotherly kindness and to brotherly kindness, charity. For if these things be in you and abound they make you that you shall neither be barren nor unfruitful in the knowledge of our Lord Jesus Christ*" (2 Peter 1:7,8).

In verse 5, it says, "*add to your faith*". I want you to really pay attention to that as we go along.

When Adam and Eve were first placed in the Garden of Eden, God had placed them there, as people who were created to be like Him. He said in the book of Genesis, "*Let Us make man in Our own image"* (Genesis 1:26).

In other words, "*Let Us create man so that he's like Us*."

Created like God.

What this meant, was that God the Father, God the Son and God the Holy Spirit first created Adam and Eve with a God nature. They had a God nature infused in them as He created them. The Bible says that He blew the breath of life into them. That means that Adam and Eve were like God.

There's something about God that has always amazed me and I've been a Christian for a lot of years. It's always amazed me that God never wants to force Himself on anyone. He's never been One who forces Himself upon people, because He is a God who functions by love and not by force. He created the Garden of Eden. It was a paradise, just a beautiful area where they had everything they needed. Everything they could possibly want was in that garden.

God allowed a tree to be placed in that garden, called the Tree of good and evil. Right from the beginning Adam and Eve always had a choice whether they served God or not. God didn't force them. They always had a choice.

Every time I read that, I think "*God, You know how human beings are; you can't give us those kinds of choices because we'll always choose the wrong thing*." But the point is, God does not want you to serve Him unless you want to serve Him. God does not want you to feel that you are forced, or burdened or under pressure. He does not want you to feel that if you don't serve Him, all hell will break loose.

But when we don't serve Him, then we remove ourselves from His protection and expose ourselves to the enemy instead. All too often hell breaking loose is what's going to happen.

God gives us a choice: choose life or death, blessing or cursing.

God gives us a choice. No one has to go to hell. *No one*! As a matter of fact, hell wasn't ever created for men. In the beginning, it was created for the devil and his angels. But because man insisted in following the devil, hell has been opened up for mankind as well.

In the Garden of Eden, Adam and Eve had everything they needed, everything anyone could ever want. But because they believed the lie of the devil, when he offered them a better life, they partook of that forbidden fruit.

We know the story. After that they were forced out of the garden. God had to tell them to leave the paradise He'd made for them. From then on they followed a different lifestyle.

Now when that happened, the spirit that God breathed in them died. When God told them, "*If you eat of this fruit you will die*." He meant that they'd die spiritually.

From then on, that spirit just lay dormant inside of Adam and Eve and all the subsequent generations of mankind. That's why Jesus came.

Jesus took the curse so we could live.

Jesus came and died on Calvary's cross so that we could come back to God. He sacrificed Himself. He took every sin that you ever committed, that I ever committed, that everyone in this world committed, past, present and future. These sins were all poured on Him on Calvary. He took all those sins as well as your punishment on Himself, so that you could be born again. Being 'born again' means that when you receive Christ, He comes and gives life to that spirit that has lain dead and dormant within us.

Our spirit becomes alive and we suddenly understand things we've never understood before. We're once again in the image and likeness of God. It's like the wires are reconnected and now we can talk to God again, knowing that He's hearing us and we're hearing Him.

In chapter one of second Peter, he makes some statements that we need to examine. He uses the word 'add'. 'Add' to your life these things. We always think of the word 'add' in the context of math. One plus one is two and so on. In this scripture however, it means something different. It means to provide – note this – to provide at your own expense.

We have to add our part…

One commentator translated it as, "adding on your part". In other words, God is saying, "*Now that I've come into your life again and saved you and set you free from the enemy, you're no longer hell bound, you're heaven bound. If you want to be productive and if you want to never get lost, then add to your life these things.*" Or, in other words, purposely bring these things into your life.

As you bring these things into your life, you will also get closer to God, closer than you've ever thought possible.

Peter said to add these things "at your own expense". What does that mean? Imagine for a moment that someone has paid the admittance price for you to get into a place. You get in and find this place is filled with food. But, you could still die of starvation inside this place if you don't eat the food that's been provided for you. If you don't understand that the price of the admittance includes the food and if you don't understand that you are now entitled to eat, because you have your admittance ticket.

What Peter means by saying, 'add these things at your own expense', is add them by your own decision, or by your own mindset, or by your own will, to your Christian life. And if you'll add them, you won't be lost. You won't have to worry about backsliding, falling away from God, or anything like that, you'll always be productive.

It's not only about you; it's also about who you can help.

You know, I was sitting the other day, and I let the Lord deal with my heart and He said this to me, "*You know I love you*," and I know God loves me, I know He does, "*but I didn't just save you just so that you and I could just sit around and love each other all the time. I saved you, and in saving and loving you the way that I do, I want you to turn around and what I've given to you; I want you to give to other people. That's what this is about. I didn't just save you for you alone. I saved you for other people as well.*"

God wants you to share what you have. He wants you to give what He's given you to someone else so that you can help other people get out of trouble.

We have people who come to our schools all the time to lecture the kids about things they should and should not do. But most of us never listen to what they say until we have learned the lesson ourselves, the hard way. Until we've been burned. Then, all of a sudden, we learn the lesson. Then we spend a lot of time trying to help people not to go down the same road.

I tell parents all the time: when you're talking to your kids, you don't have to tell them your complete past, or about all the things that you've done. But God help you, if you watch those kids making the same mistakes that you've made, and you see them headed down that same road and you never say a word, because you're too into yourself and you don't want to share with your kids. I used to be a jerk too. I used to be a jerk just like that, and that's why I'm telling you this.

There's not a whole lot my boys don't know about me. There are certain things they have no business knowing and those things they never will know. But, when I see them doing things that I've done and got into trouble with, I'm right there, telling them, "*You need to stop this because I know where you're going.*"

"*How do you know where I'm going? You don't understand.*"

"*Oh come now! I do understand. How do I understand? Let me tell you a story. Sit down.*"

When you see your kids about to make the same mistakes you've made, just say, "*I know what I'm talking about because I've been there and done the same dumb thing you're getting ready to do. And that's why I can say, don't do that.*"

We need to add virtue to our lives.

Peter says, if you want to be productive and stay saved, (and I know that we all want that,) he says; first of all add to your life, virtue. Go out and get virtue. Be a part of virtue. Virtue means 'goodness'. Now doesn't that seem a little strange?

Sometimes we Christians make things harder than they are. Peter says '*add to your life goodness.*' If Christians added goodness to their lives, we wouldn't have so many mean Christians in the world. Unfortunately, there are a lot of mean folk in the world.

"*Are you a Christian?*"

"*Oh yes...praise the Lord! If you don't get off my property I'm going to blow your head off. But I love Jesus... praise the Lord*!"

Real virtue shines like a light.

He says, '*add to your life goodness*'. God wants us to be an exemplary person in this world. That means we're to be people of courage and valor. It means that we are so full of God, that we're not afraid to share Jesus with anyone. But as we're sharing Jesus with other people, we're also living the kind of life that makes people look at us and say, "*You know what? That person's for real!*"

All of us hate phonies but all of us act phony at times! We hate lies and deceit and all those kinds of things. We hate that kind of thing, yet we act just like that at times.

God's saying, '*Add to your life goodness*'. In other words, being good to other people and living the kind of life that will never cause people to look at you and say, "*What a phony! Your Christianity's so phony. Oh you may go down to that church and raise your hands and sing and jump up and down and act like you know God, but then, you come out here and act like the devil - he's the one you really know.*"

Make them want what you've got.

God's saying through Peter, in this scripture, "*Add goodness to your life*" or "*Add power to your life.*" In practical terms, it means that you actually go out and love people to the point where people are so touched that they want what you have.

The lady that led Debbie and I to the Lord was like that. I sat and talked to her for one whole afternoon, then ate dinner with her and talked again for a few hours after dinner. I have to tell you, that by the time I walked that lady to her car and she left, I was saying to myself, "*I don't know what she's got, but I've got to have it because I can see there's a difference in her life. She has something that I don't have, that I don't possess and I've got to have it.*"

That's what this is talking about. We add goodness. We add virtue to our lives. In other words, we become full of courage. We're not afraid to share the Gospel of Jesus Christ with other people. While we're sharing it, we're living it, the best we know how.

I know you're not perfect. I'm not perfect. We all mess up and we do things we shouldn't. But, the thing is, we don't do bad things on purpose. Don't you agree?

Virtue also means moral excellence.

I was watching a television show not long ago. The interviewers were talking to a group of teenagers. They came to this one young girl and said, "*Honey, you're the only virgin on this show.*"

She smiled and said, "*I guess so…*" You know how kids are. The host said to her, "*Why are you waiting to have this experience, this sexual experience?*"

She replied, "*I want it to be with someone I know I'm going to live with the rest of my life.*"

The thing that made me mad about this program was that everybody thought it was funny that she was a virgin. That's the way the world is. That young girl's attitude demonstrated what virtue is. When Peter says, "*Add virtue to your life*" it means that we try to live a good, clean life. It means that we make a decision not to do certain things.

I always have people telling me, "*Pastor, you don't know what I'm going through because you've never been there.*" Oh honey, back it up! I've been there! I've been there and I've been there some! I've been there a little deeper than you have, perhaps! I know what I'm talking about, because I've been there. I wasn't born yesterday and I wasn't born a Christian. Some of the things I've done, I never want anyone to know about, if I can help it. But, nevertheless, I've been there. So when I say that we don't have to live like that, I know what I'm talking about.

I didn't come out of my Mom's womb going, "*Praise the Lord! Where's the church?*" You know I didn't. I've lived the worldly life too. I know the difference between the worldly life and what God has for us.

I know that we have to obey what God wants for us and live in moral excellence. We want to be able to say to our children, to people we're talking with, to people we're working with, to people who live around us, "*I'm a Christian, I love God and it's because I do love God, that I live the way I live.*"

The key to virtue is stability.

How many people are stable? When we tell people something, do we stick with what we've said? People tell me all kinds of things. Matter of fact, just this week someone told me, they'd be here in a few minutes. A few minutes turned into a half hour, then an hour. I never figured 'a few minutes' meant an hour.

Now I stop people when they tell me they'll be a couple of minutes and I ask, "*Do you know what a couple is? You just said you're going to be here in two minutes. Do you know what that means? Please, don't tell me that unless you mean that. Don't tell me that you'll meet me at five-thirty and then get here at seven-thirty. Don't waste my time.*"

Stability and consistency are a part of virtue. So is conviction. This means that when we add virtue to our lives, we don't compromise, or do bad things because someone else wants you to do them.

We have convictions that we stick to, even if it costs us.

In the Old Testament, Daniel would not eat the King's food because it was against what he believed. That's conviction. Having conviction will help you get through.

"But Daniel purposed in his heart that he would not defile himself with the portion of the king's delicacies, nor with the wine which he drank; therefore he requested of the chief of the eunuchs that he might not defile himself" (Daniel 1:8).

To have virtue, we need purification.

Another aspect of virtue is purification. We're to add purification to our hearts. When Isaiah stood in the presence of God, he just bowed down on his face because he immediately knew that his life was unclean. He couldn't help crying out to God to come and purify his heart.

One of the evidences of virtue is that we confess our faith.

As we develop virtue, we learn to live, confess and teach our faith. Paul was not ashamed of the gospel of Jesus Christ. You can find that in Romans 1:16. *"For I am not ashamed of the gospel of Christ, for it is the power of God to salvation for everyone who believes, for the Jew first and also for the Greek."*

By adding virtue, we add power to our lives. The most powerful virtue in existence is the gospel of Jesus Christ. It has power to save people, to change lives, to make things new.

That's why, as we add virtue, we're also adding more of that gospel to our lives. As we start experiencing this power, we can't help but tell other people about it. How can we keep from telling them, when we know it will help them to come out of their trouble into a good life?

CHAPTER 16
Study to Show Yourself Approved

As we exercise virtue in our lives, this develops knowledge. It's never wrong to know something. It's never wrong to learn more than you know right now.

When Peter talks about knowledge, he's not just talking about scriptural knowledge, he's also talking about knowledge that helps you grow as a Christian. How many of us really read our Bibles? How many of us not only read it, but also pray over what we've read?

When we're involved in trouble, is the scripture so real to us that we act like Christians? Do we learn from the experience? The next time we encounter trouble; do we handle it better than we did before? If we develop knowledge, then we'll know how to handle difficult situations better each time they come along. That's what 'adding knowledge' really means.

Now in Hebrews 12:12, it talks about the necessity for us to become strong and create a smooth, straight path so that the lame may not be put out of joint.

"Therefore strengthen the hands which hang down, and the feeble knees, and make straight paths for your feet, so that what is lame may not be dislocated, but rather be healed" (Hebrews 12:12).

That's adding knowledge to your

life

The lessons we learn should bring knowledge that can also help others.

Peter says, "Go *out and learn things, on purpose. Learn things that will help you live better. What you learn is not just to be used for yourself, but it should be something you can pass on to other people to help them live better, as well.*"

It would be a terrible thing if I knew that there was a big hole hidden under the mat at the entrance to my church and I didn't warn people who were coming in. If I didn't pass that knowledge on to them and instead, just watched them fall, one by one, into that hole, I would be responsible for them falling and hurting themselves.

A lot of us keep falling in holes like that all the time. Either because those who know about the hole don't warn us; or sometimes because we just never learn for ourselves how to avoid the hole in the floor, even though we've fallen into it before.

God's saying, "*I want you to learn, I want you to learn how things work. I want you to learn how life works. I want you to know what real love is.*"

Knowledge of God is knowledge of real love, unconditional love.

I've heard a lot of people talking about real love but, the truth is, most of us don't know what real love is.

Love is something that is so powerful, that if you ever get hold of what love really is, you'll never have a worry about people not liking you.

If you capture the essence of real love, people will flock around you. Real love looks at somebody and says, "*No matter what it looks like, under all that mess, I see somebody who's really good under that cover.*"

I have relatives that I look at and sometimes think, "*Lord, my God, please don't let any of this stuff come back on me. Lord I don't ever want to be like so and so.*"

I was at a party the other day and we were talking about how everyone has those relatives - that uncle in the family that everyone talks about. He lives up in one room in a part of the house and the kids always talk about the strange things he does.

"*Mom, Dad, I saw Uncle so and so... he thought he was in the bathroom but he wasn't!*" Well, everyone's got a relative like that. I have uncles and aunts like that and I always think, "*Oh Lord, please, don't let any of that rub off on me*." But there are other members of the family who look at that relative and just love them, no matter what anyone says about them, no matter what they do. You see, real love runs deep.

If God wasn't real love, none of us could be here today. We've blown our chances many times, but God's got love that runs real deep. His love covers over all those things and loves us no matter what we've done.

He says to us, "*I want you to add knowledge. Learn how to do things. If you don't know how to do something, then learn, so that you can teach others. Add knowledge to your life.*"

CHAPTER 17
Add Temperance or Self-Control

In 2 Peter 1:6, Peter goes on to talk about temperance. The word temperance means self-control. Self-control simply means the restraint of one's impulses, emotions and desires. It means that you have control of yourself. In one definition, it's said that temperance is the basis of any achievement in any field of endeavor. It's really about self-discipline.

Without self-control we get into trouble.

How many of us can say we are in control of ourselves? How many of us truly exercise self-control? Self-control is something we have to add to our Christian lives because if we don't, we get into trouble.

When Debbie and I first came to Denver, to start this church, we took a lady into our home. This girl had a penchant for stealing cheese. When she stole cheese, she would always tell me, "*Pastor, I'm not paying that, for that cheese*."

I would ask her, "*But that cheese is cold, how do you steal it?*"

She told me, "*I just put it in my pants and walk out of the store*."

And that's what she used to do.

When we'd come home and find a dish that had cheese in it, I would get mad and say, "*I'm not using that cheese*!" because I would know that she had stolen it. But she'd go on stealing and I'd keep telling her, "*You've got to stop doing that!*"

She'd say, "*Pastor, every time I walk past the cheese, I get so mad because they charge so much that I just can't help myself and I find myself stealing it.*"

That is a classic example of no self-control.

Lack of self-control shows in our words as well as our actions.

One of the Seinfeld cast was reported in another case of lack of self-control. Everybody was just crucifying him because he made some racial remarks at a comedy show. Afterwards, he said, "*I don't know how it just came out of me!*"

Now, if we find that kind of mess is just coming out of us, we'd better cap the fountain. We'd better shut it down because we've obviously got no self-control. Everyone gets mad now and then, but they don't say those kinds of things.

That kind of behavior stems from the same lack of self-control that causes men to beat up women. "*I don't know what it was, but she just kept saying stuff and it got so I couldn't take it anymore and I just smacked her.*"

That's lack of self-control. **It's allowing the anger and resentments to brew up inside until we get so mad that we can't control ourselves and we go crazy.**

When I tell you that I know what I'm talking about, this is one of the areas. I have one of those flash kinds of tempers. It takes a long time to rouse it, but when I get really mad, it explodes. Boom! Then I'm after everybody. I feel as if I could hit anybody who gets in my way. I don't care. I don't see anybody as my friend when I get like that.

But over the years I've learned, with the help of God, that kind of behavior is not Godly. It's not what He wants from me and so I've learned how to put up with stuff, instead of getting angry.

Once I decided to exercise self-control, I experienced God helping me. With His help I've learned how to control how I act and I've developed self-control over my anger. Without self-control in life, we get into trouble.

People get into all kinds of moral trouble because they've got no self-control, "*I just couldn't help myself.*" Then things start calling to us. Have you ever been in a place where things talk to you?

I'm serious. Things talk to you. I've had pie talk to me. This Thanksgiving, I went to "Heavenly Cakes" Bakery and bought a pie. When I got that pie home everyone was really looking forward to eating it, together with the two lemon meringue pies that my wife made.

They were nice pies and everyone was enjoying them. But suddenly, it seemed, the pies were gone! They were all gone. All except for a portion of a cherry pie.

I happened to walk through the kitchen and saw it sitting there. There were still a lot of people in our house. Kids and adults and they all wanted some more pie. As I'm walking through the kitchen, I heard that cherry pie say, "Norman… Nor..r…man… come here…"

I found myself standing over it, looking at the pie in the pie pan. You know how after you cut a piece, the juice kind of runs… here I am standing looking at the pie… and I'm going, "*Oh my God... pie... oooh...*"

And this is the truth: as I'm looking at it I could see my belly. I said, "*Enough pie! Enough pie!*" So I walked away and got busy doing something somewhere else, when all of a sudden, I hear it again, saying, "Norman… Norman…" The next thing I know I don't know how I got there, but the next thing I know, I'm standing looking at that pie again.

By then I had a knife in my hand. I'm cutting the pie. Not just a small slice. This is a slice you could feed three people with. By now nobody's home, but me.

So I go and sit in my red chair, put my feet up, turn on the history channel, and… eat that whole pie! Not just the first slice I cut. I went back and got the rest of it and said, "*Come with me, I'm taking you prisoner too...*" and I just ate it all! But after I ate it, guess what? You know what I'm talking about. After I ate all that pie, the guilt just rolled over me. I shouldn't have eaten that pie!

How many calories were in it? A whole lot of calories! I mean there were so many; you could start another country with all those calories! But there it is. It was too late. I said to myself, "*From now on, I'm not going to do that again!*"

Well, I won't know for sure that I won't do the same thing again until another cherry pie is there. But I can guarantee you, I've learned something and I've learned to not listen when it calls, "*Norman... come back here...*" "*No, I can't come back here.*"

You can work with God to develop self-control.

We've got to have self-control. There's got to be somewhere where you have dominion over your mind, your thoughts and your actions. You've got to get to the place where you know you can control yourself. How many of us get depressed and listen to the voices in our heads? "*Oh you're never going to make it. You're such a dog.*" It goes on and on and on.

We've got to learn to shut it down, because it's not us. We've got to learn to tell those voices to shut up and get behind us, because that's where they belong. When we have those thoughts that tell us that God doesn't love us, we've got to throw those thoughts out. We have to throw them out because they're a lie from the pit of hell.

The devil always wants us to think that God doesn't love us because if he gets us there, we'll stop trusting God. But God does love us. He loves you where you are right now and where you've been. We've got to exercise self-control and not entertain those thoughts.

If the world can do amazing feats using self-control, why can't we?

Do you enjoy watching Karate movies? It's okay, saved people can watch Karate movies. Have you ever noticed how those karate guys use their minds? When you watch them break bricks, they're not just using their fists, they're using their minds. I watched an interview with a karate guy where they asked, "*How do you break the bricks?*"

One of the things he said was, "*I see through the bricks. I see to the bottom. And when I pick up my hand and hit the stack, it goes right through, all the way down.*"

You see these guys standing on poles. They break boards. They're using mental strength. We watch this kind of thing and love it, but we don't develop mental strength like that. Our minds don't work that way. We look at the bricks and we say, "*Good Lord! That's hard! And there's ten of them there, I'm not even going to try this!*" That's how our minds work.

Throughout the scriptures, self-control is stressed. It's not the domain of the world. They don't have something that we can't have. In fact, they can never have the kind of self-control that we can develop in Christ.

God wants us to develop control over ourselves, where by having faith in Him, we *believe* that we can do anything. The truth is that when we do have faith in Him, we *can* do anything.

That's the mind control or self-control, that God wants us to have. We've got to have self-control to walk through troubles and battles and win the race. To win the prize we've got to be able to control our thinking and the way we act. If we don't, we'll never win the prize.

"*For though we walk in the flesh, we do not war according to the flesh. For the weapons of our warfare are not carnal but mighty in God for pulling down strongholds, casting down arguments and every high thing that exalts itself against the knowledge of God, bringing every thought into captivity to the obedience of Christ*" (2 Corinthians 10:3-5).

That is self-control. That is temperance. That's the evidence. When we take control of not just our actions and our words, but also our thoughts. When we don't allow any thoughts to stay in our mind that oppose what God says in His Word.

CHAPTER 18
Perserverance, Pastience, Endurance

Perseverance (steadfastness), patience, endurance. As we exercise self-control, we develop these qualities. This means that we can hold out and we don't give up.

To illustrate what I mean, let me take you through how raising a crop is planned.

You take the seed and plant it in the ground. Then you cover it and water it. That seed works it's magic. The outer shell begins to break up as the inside begins to grow. The next thing that happens is that a little blade pushes up through the ground.

If it was a corn seed that was planted, and someone goes and digs up that little plant as soon as it's sticking up out of the ground, it's pretty obvious that you won't get any corn. Why? Because, there's no corn on the plant yet. But you can have leaf tonight if you want. You can boil up that little leaf and see if it'll feed you. If you'd rather eat corn you're going to have to have the patience to let the plant grow up.

If you leave it in the ground long enough, you'll see the blade push through, then you'll see the little spears appear and they'll begin to develop into a bigger plant. If you cut the plant down at that stage, you'll be able to boil the leaves and the stalk, but you'll still have no corn. But if you have a little more patience and endurance, enough to let that plant grow up into a corn stalk and you continue to wait for it to develop its fruit before you pick it, you'll have corn.

Life's not fair…

That's what this verse means. It's saying "*go out and get endurance or patience*." In other words, stop being a cry-baby. There are some tough cry-babies out there.

Some people are really tough on the outside, but they're still cry-babies. Always whining about something. Always saying, "*Well I don't have... Well I've been cheated.*"

Little kids are notorious for saying things like, "*That's not fair!*" Well honey, life isn't fair. Life never has been fair. And if you don't trust God enough to see you through until you get the fruit, you're never going to survive or make it in this life.

That's what happens with a lot of people. They receive Christ and they're so overjoyed about living for God at the time. But later the first time they run into trouble, they backslide and go back to their old ways and to what they were doing before. That's because they've got no patience, no endurance. They haven't developed that in their lives. You cannot be a Christian and stay a Christian if you have no endurance.

Life can be tough. Life can be horrible. Life can throw you some real bad curves, but you've got to be man enough or woman enough, to stand up and say, "*God I'm still here, I'm still alive, and I'm going to trust you no matter what.*" That's how you get the fruit.

Most people don't do that. Most people give up when trouble comes.

You can't endure or persevere if you're easily offended.

I've pastored churches for many years and I've seen people leave churches because someone looked at them wrong. What's spiritual about that?

"*Well you know I was sitting in this church and I looked over and he was giving me those crusty looks, so I don't want to come here anymore.*"

What! You're leaving because of what!?

I've had people leaving the church because I was taking an offering and they thought I wanted all their money! If I wanted all their money, I'd go and get a gun and rob them and take all their money! "*Oh I don't want to go to that church!*"

I've had people say, "*I don't want to go to that church because there's too many minorities in that church.*" What!? Where's the Christian spirit here? Where is it? I don't understand this. How do people say they're Christians and yet say things like that?

At one time, when Debbie and I pioneered our first church, I had several wives come to me. They with their husbands were all getting ready to leave the church. I asked them what was wrong. The trouble was that there was one lady who was coming to church wearing really short dresses. She was a new Christian, and to this day I think she just didn't understand yet about dressing modestly.

She'd always come and sit close to the platform and cross her legs. And when she'd cross her legs, you could see all the men on the platform struggling with this. I was seeing them struggle with this. Their wives were seeing them struggling with this and so they came to me and they said, "*Pastor we're just going to leave this church, because, that woman, oh Lord, she's just going to mess our men up*!"

I said, "*Wait a minute! Wait a minute. First of all, maybe the lady just doesn't realize what she's doing. At least let me talk with her and see what we can do.*" Then I continued, "*But the real deal is, you need to talk to your husbands. Tell them to quit looking.*" Pretty soon, the lady cleaned up her act and she did fine.

Spiritual maturity comes through endurance.

Many church people talk about being spiritual, but really, they've got no endurance.

"*Why are you quitting God?*"

"*Because He didn't answer my prayer.*"

Well, what have you done for God?

"*Well he was too late. It took Him too long to come through and help me."*

No. That's not the way it works. We've got to have endurance to stay the course.

My wife and I were talking about how long we've been married. We've been married so long we've learned how to deal with one another. We've learned how to endure each other. There are times when all I've got to do is talk to her and she'll give me a look and I'll know where she's at and I say, "*Hey, I'll see you in about a half hour*."

When we learn how to work with one another and how to endure, then there's fruit. I've reaped a lot of fruit in my life and I wouldn't trade my life for anything.

Why? Because it's been a good life. It's been a good life because God has taught me how to stay with it and trust Him until He brought me through. And he's always brought me through.

He'll bring you through too, if you develop perseverance, patience and endurance.

CHAPTER 19

Godliness - Don't Mess With Big Trucks

Now let me go on. Peter says that as we exercise endurance, we will develop 'Godliness'. What is Godliness?

I found this quote. I wish it was my own saying, but it's not. It says this, "I have a rule about driving. Don't mess with buses and large trucks."

Now why is that good advice? Because buses and large trucks can run you over. So what should you do? You should respect them. In other words, you pull your little Volkswagen Beetle, black with nice rims on, out of the way and don't let the buses or large trucks run over you.

It's the same way with God. We don't mess with something we can't handle. We have honor and respect for God, because if God ever gets after us, we're not going to get away. If God's our enemy then we'd better give up now, because we're dead! You might as well give up.

Godliness is just having respect for God and doing what God wants you to do, or doing what pleases God. That's 'Godliness'.

What you're doing right now pleases God. As you're reading it's pleasing God because we're talking about His Word. It's pleasing to Him. He enjoys that. When you pray it's pleasing God. When you help other people it's pleasing God. God looks at those things you do and He strengthens and builds you up and adds more to you because you act like that.

CHAPTER 20

Brotherly Kindness - It's What The World Sees

One of the last qualities Peter discusses in 2 Peter 1:7 is brotherly kindness. He says that as we exercise Godliness, we're to also exercise brotherly kindness, which will in turn develop Christian love.

In Ephesians 4:31,32 , it says, "*Be ye kind to one another, tender hearted, forgiving one another even as God, for Christ's sake hath forgiven you.*"

The Lord is our great demonstration. Jesus is our great example. When a woman who was caught in adultery came to Him, there was a law that any woman caught in fornication, as she was, should be stoned to death. That was the Biblical law. That was the law in that culture at that time.

But you know what Jesus did? He went beyond that law and forgave her. Why? Because He felt her pain and her hurt and He saw why she was there. He saw how she had become that way and He had compassion for her. That's brotherly kindness.

In the book of Revelations, the Bible talks about a church in Philadelphia. Philadelphia is a Greek word and it means 'brotherly love'. The city of Philadelphia in the United States is named the city of 'brotherly love'.

What does brotherly love mean?

What does brotherly love mean? It means that you love people around you. The Bible says you're not going to stay stable and productive unless you learn how to love people that are around you.

Isn't it funny how we always like to love everybody in Africa? And we love to love everybody in Asia and in Egypt and all those other faraway places.

But nobody wants to love the person next door.
There's something wrong with that.

"*Well I love to love people that can't come and bother me.*" That's what you need to say. "*I'm going to send that $50 over there so that person will stay over there.*" Huh!?

But the Bible says we're to exercise brotherly kindness. That means that we're to love people in our own church. In our own neighborhood.

Uh oh! In *this* church? In *this* neighborhood? There are some 'different' people in this church, in this neighborhood.

Yes. That's what it means. It means you love the people right here, where you live.

"*Yeah but you know what? There are problems...*"

Yeah, but you know what, that woman caught in adultery had a problem too! Jesus overlooked what she'd done, to love and reach her. Then He didn't just say, "*Hey you sinned, just forget it, I'll take it, just get out of here...*"

No, he said, "*Where are your accusers? No-one's here to accuse you. Neither do I accuse you. But... don't keep living like that.*" That is what He told her.

We need to understand that God is kind. Throughout both the New and Old Testaments, there are scriptures like we see here in Nehemiah 9:17

"*But You are God, ready to pardon, Gracious and merciful, Slow to anger, Abundant in kindness, And You did not forsake them...*"

In the first century church, Christians were known by their love – the kind and tender affection they held for one another.

It was Jesus' prayer that we would love one another as He has loved us and that all men would know that we are His disciples by the love we have for one another. You can read this in John Chapters 13 and 15.

That's the kind of love that He wants us to add to our lives.

CHAPTER 21
The Bottom Line

The bottom line is that if we're going to live for God, if we want to stay saved, and see fruit in our lives and see Him working, then these things that Peter lists are essential.

These are not things that we wait for the Holy Spirit to give us. We have to work at developing them in our lives. When we do the Holy Spirit will help us, but He's saying, "*Go out and begin developing these yourself. Make the effort yourself.*"

Peter tells us to add: virtue or goodness, knowledge, self control, patience or endurance, Godliness and brotherly kindness. It's all there in 2 Peter 1:1-8.

If we're going to live for God, these are things that we've got to develop in our lives. And they're not something we get one time and we're done. Note that in Verse 8, it says we're to possess them '*in increasing measure*.' This means that we've got to continually work on growing these qualities in us. real Christianity is about growth, effectiveness and productivity.

I'd like to challenge you to study the word of God. For the next few days, keep reading 2 Peter 1. Read it over and over again. It will change your life.

If you really get a grip on it, it will change your life. Because it will show you what real Christianity is all about. It's about having all those qualities evident in your life, so evident that other people see them.

That's real Christianity. Sometimes, I get into trouble because I tell people, "*Your Christianity isn't showing.*"

People judge us by how we act and how we present ourselves. And all too often, the Christianity isn't showing.

Why isn't it showing? It's not showing because these things that Peter tells us to get are missing.

Now if you've just recently received the Lord, perhaps while you were reading this book, don't get condemned. The Lord will help you. But even as a new believer, it's your responsibility to develop these things in your life as well.

These are the things that God's telling you to add to your life to keep you strong. Do you want to be strong before the Lord? Do you want to see God do powerful things? He'll do that today if you'll do your part.

To help you do your part, go through the study guide provided after this chapter. If you're not already attending a strong church that preaches the Word of God, find one in your area and go there to be taught. If you need help finding one, please email rolchuch@aol.com and we'll help you find one.

STUDY GUIDE
Part One

Two Ways to Travel:

In Part One we saw that there are two ways to travel:

1. naturally (in the boat, in bondage to fear)
2. supernaturally (walking on water… walking on top of trouble into triumph)

In this part of the study guide, we'll be studying how to:

Walk on the Water

To anchor you in faith I have created an acronym that will help you remember to stay focused.

W - Willingness

A – Attitude or Alertness

T – Truth (what is the)

E – Excitement (of the new)

R – Revelation

Willingness:

You have to have the motivation to choose between being afraid and remaining strong.

1. **Look in a Bible concordance** and see how many times in the New Testament the phrase, "*be not afraid*" or "*fear not*" is used.

2. **Read Matthew 14: 27.** The Greek word 'Phobeo' used in the original text, which is translated as 'afraid' in this verse means:

a. put to flight

b. struck with fear

c. seized with alarm

All of these meanings have one thing in common: they *immobilize* you!

3. **Read Numbers 13:30-33** and note all the obstacles the men *choose to look at.*

4. What did Caleb say that made it obvious that he had a willingness to win?

Attitude:

In verse Matthew 14:31 Jesus said to Peter, "*Wherefore didst thou doubt?*"

Doubt is an attitude that says, "*You can do this but I can't. You are better equipped than I am, therefore I am sinking.*"

1. **To develop the right attitude** you must remember that you have been invited to accomplish the supernatural.

a. Jesus said, "Come" - Matthew 14: 29.

b. Look at John 14:12, Matthew 10:8

2. **To maintain the right attitude** you must remember Jesus commands us not to fear and not to doubt

a. As Jesus is sending his disciples out to minister he tells them, "Fear not" - Matthew 10:31 (Read this Chapter.)

b. If the disciples were in fear they would not be able to accomplish his goals for them

Truth:

Jesus instructed his disciples to go to the other side of the sea.

When God has given us his word we need to depend on it as truth.

1. Read Titus 1:2 and Hebrews 6:18

2. John 17:17 says, *"Sanctify them through Thy truth: Thy Word is truth."*

The Greek word 'Hagiazo' used in the original text, which is translated as 'Sanctify' means to:

i. to purify by expiation: free from the guilt of sin[3]

ii.to purify internally by renewing of the soul

iii.This happens through meditating on the Word which brings correction and guidance

3. Read 2 Timothy 3:16

Excitement:

The new experience of walking on the water is what got Peter out of the boat.

1. Isaiah 43:19 "*Behold, I will do a new thing now it shall spring forth shall ye not know it? I will even make a way in the wilderness and rivers in the desert.*"

a. God is saying to the Israelites that their deliverance out of Babylon would be more famous than their deliverance from Egypt

b. Deliverance from the old always brings joy!

2. Read Luke 24:17-32

a. Notice what they said in verse 32. This is the kind of excitement from God that gives you hope to look forward to a new day.

3. Explain what you see in Acts 3:1-9.

Revelation:

A manifestation of divine will or truth[4]

Jesus can walk on water. If Jesus says we are to do something, we can walk on the water or any trouble to the successful achievement of His command. If we are trusting Jesus, He will take us safely to the other side in any storm.

These are all revelations that will strengthen us for the future.

1. Example of a Revelation that strengthened: 2 Kings 6:15-17

2. Read 1John 4:4. How it make you feel to know this fact?

How will what you've learned affect the decisions you make from now on?

Make a summary of what you have learned from this Part One of the book and study guide. Refer to this daily.

STUDY GUIDE
Part Two

Do you see Jesus?

In Part Two, we saw how critical it is for us to 'see Jesus' even in the midst of our trials. We have to be willing to lay aside all the distractions and truly focus on Him and what He's saying to us in His Word. This section of the study guide will help you to understand more about this.

Focus on Him

To anchor you in faith I have created an acronym that will help you remember to stay focused.

F – focus (on Him)

O – outlook

C – confidence (in Him)

U – undivided (heart)

S – see (Him)

Focus:

Mary willingly chooses to sit at Jesus' feet. She is focusing her attention on Him. We cannot have faith *in* Him if we don't focus *on* Him.

1. **Read Hebrews 11:6** "*But without faith it is impossible to please him: for he that cometh to God must believe that he is, and that he is a rewarder of them that diligently seek him.*"

a. What things in your life keep you from hearing the voice of Jesus?

2. **Read Numbers 22:22-35** after reading the story of Balaam do you feel a connection because you sense you're headed the wrong way in life?

a. Take note of some of the dangers of wanting to promote your agenda over God's

b. Look at these Key Points the lead in the right direction

i. The importance of Focus - James 1:8

ii. Take the initiative in drawing near to God -James 4:8

Outlook:

...Balaam's anger was kindled and he smote the ass with a staff - Numbers.22:27

1. Balaam's outlook was colored by anger. Why? Because the way he saw it, the donkey was mocking him! His outlook prevented him from seeing God at work.

a. In his estimation the donkey was making a fool of him

b. A negative, angry outlook will prevent us hearing from God

c. Balaam's comrades: Genesis 4:5-6, Luke 15: 25-32

2. Who or what would you consider a donkey that talks in your life?

3. Martha thought the Lord didn't care because His agenda differed from hers.

a. Read Luke 10:40

b. State the areas in your life where it seems the Lord doesn't care

Confidence:

God's agenda is what matters most! We need to be confident in His care of us, so that we can wholeheartedly pursue His agenda, knowing that if we do so, it give us access to His blessings.

1. **Matthew 6:33** *"But seek ye first the kingdom of God and his righteousness and all these things shall be added unto you."*

a. Keys in following God's agenda

i. Read Proverbs 3:6 and Psalms 119:105

ii. Mary did what was needful

- Sat and heard the Word

- Chose the good

- Invested in something that could not be taken away.

b. Write down things that seem most important in your life. Being honest do you feel they fall in line with God's agenda or are they off track?

Undivided:

We will only see Jesus if our hearts are undivided. Seeing Jesus brings joy and excitement in our lives.

1. **Read the story** about the woman at the well in John 4:29 "*Come see a man which told me all things that ever I did - is this not the Christ?*"

a. Really seeing Jesus develops a confidence that all things are possible.

b. Seeing Him develops endurance.

i. Job endured because he could see. Read Job19:25

2. **If you knew you could not lose, how would you live**?

Hebrews 12:2 (The Message) says, "*Keep your eyes on Jesus, who both began and finished this race we're in. Study how he did it. Because he never lost sight of where he was headed - that exhilarating finish in and with God - he could put up with anything along the way: cross, shame, what-*

ever. And now he's there, in the place of honor, right alongside God."

See:

Jesus can be close but powerless, if we don't see Him and trust in Him with confidence.

1. Read Hebrews 11:6 - Faith is the language of God

a. He champions those that walk on top of unbelief

b. Read Matthew 15:22-28 and write down the reason the mother was successful

Make a summary of what you have learned from Part Two of the book and study guide. Add this to the summary from Part One. Refer to this daily.

STUDY GUIDE
Part Three

The Odds Don't Matter:

In Part Three of 'Two Ways to Travel', we recognize that with God's participation in our lives, we can overwhelm the odds, no matter how big or overwhelming they may seem.

In this part of the study guide, we'll be studying how to use the acronym: 'Odds'

O - Obedience

D - Departure

D - Deliverance

S - Strength

Obedience:

Obedience is often overlooked as a powerful key in serving God.

In Judges 6:1 we read, "And *the children of Israel did evil in the eyes of the Lord...*" The evil was disobedience. Notice in verse 1 "*and the Lord delivered them*"... into the hands of the Midianites.

1. "Delivered" in this verse, means 'to grant' or 'to give over to'. God gave them over to the consequences of their own choices.

2. **Read Romans 1:18-24**

3. Because of the choices the Israelites made, they found themselves under the bondage of the Midianites – remember that the word 'Midianite' means strife or contention. The word contention can mean 'justifying', 'reasoning' or 'a line of argument'.

4. In the story of King Saul in **1 Samuel 15** what is God's desire for Saul (verse 22)? Can you see how justifying your choice over God's will can be dangerous and prevent you from reaching and fulfilling the destiny God has prepared for you?

5. According to **Romans 6:16** who and what you're obedient to has a profound impact on you.

   a. What is this impact?

   b. Can you identify bad and / or good things that have happened in your life as a result of decisions you've made?

   c. According to **Hebrews 5:8** how did Jesus learn obedience?

6. The fact that Gideon obeys God brings great benefit to him and to the lives of the Israelites. What are some of these benefits?

Departure:

Departure can remove you from the path of things that bring you harm.

My wife and I celebrated our 36th anniversary by taking a cruise to the Caribbean. When we booked the cruise, we didn't realize that we'd booked it for during the hurricane season. However, the departure was timed to avoid the hurricane – the storm was either ahead of us or behind us. Because of the time of departure, and the wisdom of the captain of the ship, we had a glorious trip!

Gideon had to *see himself* a leader even though his clothes were worn and his stomach was growling. *He had to depart from the despair and see himself differently.*

1. **Where is your focus?** Psalms 23:4, says "*Yea, though I walk through the valley of the shadow of death I will fear no evil for thou art with me; thy rod and thy staff they comfort me*

a. Notice the words: '*through*', '*no fear*', '*with*' and '*comfort*'.

b. We are always to be in the position of departing from the valley - we don't dwell there. We are not to fear so we must depart from the fear and move towards the Lord. We have to remember that Someone is *always* with us: the Holy Spirit.

c. The rod is a symbol of authority and there is no authority greater than our God. The Bible says in Ephesians 1:20-22 that Christ has been exalted above all rule and dominion and power and authority and every name that is named or that ever will be named.

d. The staff represents support (of every kind) so we know we'll have comfort, if we focus on Him, trusting Him. We have to focus on these facts – we must do more than just acknowledge them, we have to walk in these facts!

2. We must depart from the view we carry of ourselves and adhere to God's view of us

a. **Review Judges 6:12**.

b. What is this verse saying to you?

c. How does **Romans 8:37** correlate with this verse?

d. **Looking at Romans 4:17** from the Message translation what made Abraham a stand out?

"We call Abraham "father" not because he got God's attention by living like a saint, but because God made something out of Abraham when he was a nobody. Isn't that what we've always read in Scripture, God saying to Abraham, "I set you up as father of many peoples"? Abraham was first named "father" and then became a father because he dared to trust God to do what only God could do: raise the dead to life, with a word make something out of nothing."

3. We always 'depart' to God - not away from Him

Remember in Judges, Gideon's elders had departed from God and it was this departure that had caused the Israelites to become impoverished.

However when we turn back to God, departing from those things that separate us from Him, He won't deny us, He will draw near to us.

Deliverance:

God will send a prophet with a plan that will guide you to freedom.

1. Jesus coming and dying on the cross is prophesied in **John 3:16** and **Isaiah 53:10**.

   a. Moses was called to deliver the Israelites in **Exodus 3:16-22**

   b. God sent Paul's deliverance through Ananias in **Acts 9:1-15**

   c. In the Book of Judges, God always raised a man or woman (**Judges 4:4**) to deliver those under bondage

2. The role of the Christian can change from being delivered, to becoming the deliverer. Gideon was delivered from his inadequacy to become the deliverer of his nation.

   a. When you read **Matthew 28:19-20** what role do you see for your life?

Strength:

Strength comes in Balance. In Acts 3:16 a lame man is healed. All the people around are astounded by this act of the disciples. But before it gets out of hand, Peter brings everything into perspective and says, "*By faith in the name of Jesus, this man whom you see and know was made strong. It is Jesus' name and the faith that comes through him that has given this complete healing to him, as you can all see.*"

The disciples prayed the prayer of faith but the Holy Spirit did the work.

1. Remember, in Chapter 10 of this book we learned that whenever we take a step away from the Lord, we're taking a step down.

   a. Samson loses his strength in **Judges 16:20** because he lost what?

   b. **Matthew 19:26** speaks of adoption. What do you see as the benefits of this relationship?

2. What does God say about the gods of the Amorites in **Judges 6:10?**

3. Can fear and faith dominate at the same time? **Romans 8:15**

4. What is the problem with having two opinions?

5. Why is **decision** a powerful part of serving God? **1 Kings 18:21**

6. How does **John 15:5** relate to God telling Gideon to "*go in thy (his) might*"?

a. Look what God told Moses when Israel was trapped at the Red sea **Exodus 14:15**. What does this tell you about His part and Moses' part? What does it tell you about His part and your part?

b. How would you reconcile the two concepts: "*Go in thy might*" and "*without me you can do nothing*"?

Make a summary of what you have learned from Part Three of the book and study guide. Add this to the summary from Parts One, and Two. Refer to this daily.

STUDY GUIDE
Part Four

The Proof of Real Christianity:

In Part four we see that we are responsible for how strong our Christian Life will be based on how much attention, thought and adherence we give to the Word of God.

In this part of the study guide, we'll be studying how to use the acronym:

P - Promises

R - Responsibility

O - Officiate

O - Overcome

F - Faith

Promises:

"Whereby are given unto us exceeding great and precious promises that by these ye might be partakers of the divine nature having escaped the corruption that is in the world through lust" **(2 Peter 1:4).**

1. To live a strong life in Christ we have to actually apply the promises God has provided for us in His word. We cannot simply read them, we need to believe them and act on them. The Bible is a practical instruction manual for living. It is not theoretical, or just 'good suggestions' or simply inspirational to make us feel good for a few moments while we read it.

2. Read 2 Timothy 3:16

a. This verse says that all scripture is '*inspired*' (KJV) by God, or '*God breathed' and 'profitable for instruction, for reproof and conviction of sin, for correction of error and discipline in* ***obedience and for training in righteousness in holy living****, in conformity to God's will, in thought, purpose and action.*'

b. What level of importance do you habitually give the Word in your daily actions, thoughts and speech? Do you routinely apply the Word to the things you do every day? List ways that you could do this and the difference it could make in your life.

c. Application, or 'doing the Word' is a must. The Bible is God speaking to you. When you read the Word, imagine Jesus sitting with you and actually speaking these scriptures to you as directives for your day (and life).

Responsibility

Read the story in 2 Kings 13, pay close attention to verses 14-19

1. Who was responsible for the number of years of victory Israel had?

2. Go back and look at the meaning of "Add to" in 2 Peter 1 as discussed in Chapter 15.

a. In order to mature in this life, we have to make an effort to co-operate with God. He gives us all we need in order to mature. But if we don't consciously lay hold of and use what He gives us; what He has given us will do us no good. There must be effort on our part to develop maturity.

Read the story of Noah in Genesis 6 and answer these questions:

1. Noah already had favor with God, but what did Noah have to *do* to save himself and his family?

2. In verses 14-17 what is God giving Noah?

3. Did Noah have any option about obeying what God said?

4. Why was it important for Noah to listen to God?

Officiate

To officiate means to manage your life or to be in control of a process or event. If you abdicate your responsibility to be in control, and do not make decisions that will result in good, something or someone else will step into the gap and they will take control, making decisions that result in bad outcomes.

1. Read Genesis 3:6. What did Adam do that was a mistake?

a. **Joshua 24:15** "*And if it seem evil unto you to serve the LORD choose you this day whom ye will serve ; whether the gods which your fathers served that were on the other side of the flood or the gods of the Amorites in whose land ye dwell: but as for me and my house we will serve the LORD.*"

b. How could this Old Testament scripture apply to your life today?

c. **Read James 1:8** and write down what parallels you see between the two verses as regards decision making.

2. Read John 6:53-69 why did some of the disciples leave Jesus in this chapter? How does this chapter relate to Matthew 13:1-8?

a. What correlation do you see between what you believe and the decisions you make?

b. In what ways have your beliefs influenced decisions you've made, or not made?

c. Have you ever made decisions based on wrong beliefs?

Overcome

"*Ye are of God little children and have overcome them because greater is He that is in you than he that is in the world*" **(1 John 4:4).**

1. **We are destined to be overcomers** because of who God is and because He is in us once we ask Jesus into our hearts. It is not dependent on our ability, but in our deciding to believe what God says about us, then acting on what He says.

a. After reading **Luke 11:22, John 16:33** and **Romans 12:21** what should be your attitude about giving in to the trials you face in life?

2. Knowledge and vision are key to becoming an overcomer. **Read 2 Kings 6:8-17**

a. How do you feel when you take a test for which you know you have studied and are prepared?

b. What is your attitude when you know you have all the tools to win?

c. What difference would it make in your daily life if you knew that God had provided every tool you needed to win in every situation?

d. How will you go about finding out what tools God has given you?

Faith

"But without faith it is impossible to please Him, for he that cometh to God must believe that He is and that He is a rewarder of them that diligently seek Him" **(Hebrews 11:6).**

1. **Spiritually mature Christians understand that "faith" is the language of God**

a. Read examples of great faith in **Matthew 8:5-10** and **Matthew 15: 22-28.**

b. After reading these examples what measures could you take to strengthen your faith?

c. What are some of the things that you have previously allowed to weaken your faith? How would you handle these situations today with the knowledge you now have?

Make a summary of what you have learned from Part Four of the book and study guide. Add this to the summary from Parts One, Two and Three. Refer to this daily until you become established and disciplined in faith.

ABOUT
Rev. Norman E. Moon

Norman E. Moon is Senior Pastor at River of Life Church in Denver, Colorado.

His heart is to encourage and motivate people to pursue a passionate relationship with God. **'Two Ways to Travel'**, his first book is based on a collection of sermons preached at River of Life.

Pastor Norman's passion and excitement for God is evident. An accomplished communicator, able to reach people of all ages and walks of life, he has ministered throughout the United States and internationally.

In addition to preaching and teaching, Pastor Norman is also a prolific songwriter

Norman Moon received his Biblical Studies degree from the Nazarene College, Colorado Springs, Colorado in 1976.

He has been ministering for over 25 years both as a pastor and in other capacities. His life has focused on helping people.

Besides pastoring, he has been involved in Promise Keepers, and worked as a Family Advocate for both the Colorado Federation of Families for Children's Mental Health and Vroon Vandenberg, a consulting firm specializing in the 'Wraparound Process'.

Pastor Norman Moon has been

married to his wife, Debbie, for over 39 years. They have three sons, Aaron, Anthony and Michael, and six grandchildren: granddaughters Tyler, Nyla, Erin and grandsons Alonzo, Elijah and Michael Jr.

To find out more about Pastor Moon, or to purchase copies of this book, please visit the Norman Moon Ministries web site: www.moonministries.com.

To schedule Pastor Moon for speaking engagements, or to inquire about retail rates, please email him at lipsterbig@aol.com.

FOOTNOTES

1. Wikipedia contributors, "Doubt," Wikipedia, The Free Encyclopedia, http://en.wikipedia.org/w/index.php?title=Doubt&oldid=246630585 (accessed October 21, 2008).

2. "The Man Who Refused to Quit" Pastor Stephen Daily, www.Shadycrest.org/sojerq.htm

3. Crosswalk Bible Study Tools

4. The American Heritage® Dictionary of the English Language: Fourth Edition. 2000.

Printed in the United States
134574LV00004B/2/P